# The Best of The Mailbox®
# Bulletin Boards Book 2

## Table of Contents

# About This Book

Packed with loads of our most popular bulletin boards for preschool and kindergarten teachers, *The Best of* The Mailbox® *Bulletin Boards—Book 2* is the perfect resource for creating an inviting classroom! Inside you'll find more than 100 motivating and easy-to-create displays compiled from *The Mailbox*® line of magazines and books.

Organized by season, this handy resource includes displays for fall, winter, spring and summer, and a special collection for any day of the year. A wide array of patterns accompany the boards, saving you valuable time in creating and setting up your displays. Use the boards to supplement instruction, manage your classroom, and display student work. *The Best of* The Mailbox® *Bulletin Boards—Book 2* is the best resource for an eye-catching classroom!

**Managing Editor:** Cindy Daoust
**Editor at Large:** Diane Badden
**Copy Editors:** Tazmen Carlisle, Amy Kirtley-Hill, Kristy Parton, Debbie Shoffner, Cathy Edwards Simrell
**Cover Artist:** Clevell Harris
**Art Coordinator:** Theresa Lewis Goode
**Contributing Graphics Coordinator:** Cathy Spangler Bruce
**Artists:** Pam Crane, Chris Curry, Shane Freeman, Theresa Lewis Goode, Clevell Harris, Ivy L. Koonce, Clint Moore, Greg D. Rieves, Rebecca Saunders, Barry Slate, Stuart Smith, Donna K. Teal
**The Mailbox® Books.com:** Judy P. Wyndham (MANAGER); Jennifer Tipton Bennett (DESIGNER/ARTIST); Karen White (INTERNET COORDINATOR); Paul Fleetwood, Xiaoyun Wu (SYSTEMS)

**President, The Mailbox Book Company™:** Joseph C. Bucci
**Director of Book Planning and Development:** Chris Poindexter
**Curriculum Director:** Karen P. Shelton
**Book Development Managers:** Cayce Guiliano, Elizabeth H. Lindsay, Thad McLaurin
**Editorial Planning:** Kimberley Bruck (DIRECTOR); Debra Liverman, Sharon Murphy, Susan Walker (TEAM LEADERS)
**Editorial and Freelance Management:** Karen A. Brudnak; Sarah Hamblet, Hope Rodgers (EDITORIAL ASSISTANTS)
**Editorial Production:** Lisa K. Pitts (TRAFFIC MANAGER); Lynette Dickerson (TYPE SYSTEMS); Mark Rainey (TYPESETTER)
**Librarian:** Dorothy C. McKinney

## www.themailbox.com

Manufactured in the United States
10 9 8 7 6 5 4 3 2 1

# Fall

# A PICTURE-PERFECT CLASS!

To create this display, use the **camera pattern** (page 81) to make a construction paper camera for each child. Cut each pattern where indicated. Tape a different child's photograph behind each lens opening. Then tape a small piece of foil behind the flash opening. Display the cameras with the title "A Picture-Perfect Class!"

Laura Cozzi—Gr. K
Truman School

Here's a bright idea to welcome your new batch of students! Bring several old pairs of sunglasses to school. On the first day, photograph students in groups of two or three wearing the sunglasses. Duplicate the **sunglasses pattern** (page 82) on different colors of construction paper for students to cut out. Attach the photographs to the sunglasses patterns; then mount them on the board with a large cut-out sun.

Start the year on a "beary" positive note! Duplicate the **teddy bear pattern** (page 83) on construction paper for each child. Cut out and label each bear with a student's name. Also cut out a speech bubble from white paper for each student. Mount the bears and speech bubbles as shown on the bulletin board. Later in the week have each child tell about one thing that makes him special. Write his comment in the speech bubble above his bear.

Youngsters' contributions will add a colorful touch to this door display. Before the first day of school, send each child an introductory letter along with a personalized **crayon pattern** (page 84) cut from white construction paper. Ask each student to color, paint, or otherwise decorate the crayon shape his favorite color and bring it to school on the first day. After using the crayons for various activities, mount them onto a door covered with brightly colored paper.

Sandy Whicker—3-year-olds
Kernersville Moravian Preschool
Kernersville, NC

This preschool puzzle shows parents how your class fits together! Using the pieces of a large floor puzzle as patterns, cut interlocking puzzle pieces from colorful construction paper. To each paper puzzle piece, attach a child's photo and a real, personalized puzzle piece. Have students embellish the pieces with glitter if desired. Arrange the pieces together on a bulletin board, along with a border of real puzzle pieces. Finish off this display with the title "We Fit Together."

Cindy Bormann—Preschool, Small World Preschool, West Bend, IA

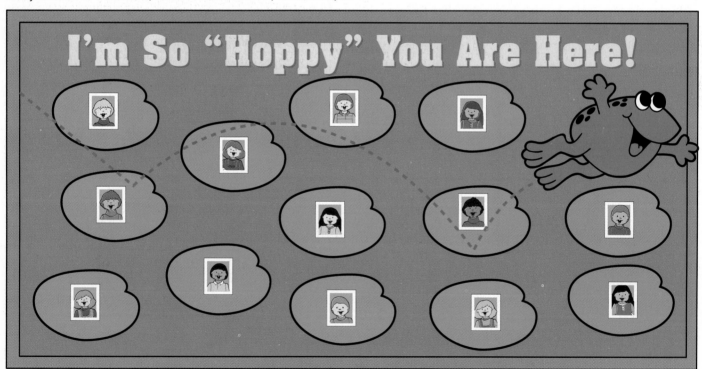

Welcome students to your "pad" with this cheerful display. Enlarge the frog pattern (page 85); then color it, cut it out, and mount it on the board. (For a 3-D touch, glue a piece of sponge to the back of the frog; then glue the sponge to the bulletin board.) Duplicate the **lily pad pattern** (page 85) onto green construction paper for each child. Cut out each lily pad. Ask children to bring in photos of themselves to mount on the lily pads. What a "hoppy" way to say hello!

Use the **toaster pattern** (page 86) to create an aluminum foil toaster with construction paper details. Mount the cutout onto a bulletin board. For each child, mount a personalized **toast pattern** (page 86) cutout near the toaster. Take a candid picture of each child participating in a different activity in the room. Attach a developed photo to each child's toast shape. For a terrific twist, replace existing photos with pictures taken on a field trip or while participating in a special outdoor activity.

Tanya Bator—Toddler Teacher, Mont Marie Childcare Center, Holyoke, MA

Show others how much fun and learning have taken place in your room by decorating a bulletin board with photos from the previous school year. Write a caption for each photo on a **space-related pattern** (page 87) cutout and then attach it near the picture. Welcome your new students with the title "Kindergarten Is a Blast." Your new kindergartners will be excited to see what they will be doing.

Marcia Longo—Gr. K, Hancock North Central Elementary, Pass Christian, MS

Let new students know that you're glad that they'll be "hanging around" your class this year! Duplicate the **T-shirt pattern** (page 88) on white construction paper for each child. Have the student cut out, personalize, and decorate his shirt. Use a permanent marker to label a white cotton T-shirt as shown. Display the shirts using clothespins and lengths of heavy string or plastic clothesline.

Twist brown bulletin board paper; then mount it on a sky blue background so that it resembles a tree and branches. Personalize an **apple pattern** (page 89) cutout for each child; then attach a photo of each child to his cutout. Attach the apples to the branches along with green leaf cutouts. Title the board to complete a delicious Open House display. Later remove and laminate the apple cutouts. Attach magnetic tape to the backs to create magnets well worth picking!

Lynn Cadogan, Starkey Elementary, Seminole, FL

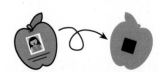

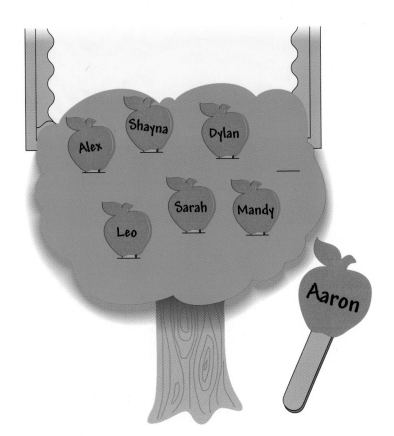

An apple a day teaches youngsters name recognition and responsibility and helps you with attendance! For each child, glue a personalized red poster board apple shape to a craft stick (**apple pattern** on page 89). To make a tree, cut a piece of green poster board to resemble the top of the tree; then cut as many slits (wide enough for the craft sticks) in the tree as you have children in your class. Mount the top of the tree to the bottom of a bulletin board so that students can insert and take out the apples easily. On the wall, mount a trunk cut from Con-Tact paper that resembles wood grain. When a child arrives each day, he "picks" his apple and gives it to the teacher. As the seasons change, replace the apples with leaves, then snowflakes, then flower blossoms!

Kathleen Palovcak—Three-Year-Olds
Bensalem Christian Day School
Bensalem, PA

This door display is the pick of the crop for welcoming youngsters! Cover the door with paper; then add a border of apple cutouts (**apple pattern** on page 89). On a large apple cutout labeled "Welcome," glue large pom-poms and a pair of wiggle eyes stickers to resemble a worm. Add the apple to the door along with students' personalized, sponge-painted apple cutouts. What an appealing door display!

adapted from an idea by Alicia Mia
  Dillingham—Pre-K
Denbigh Early Childhood Center
Newport News, VA

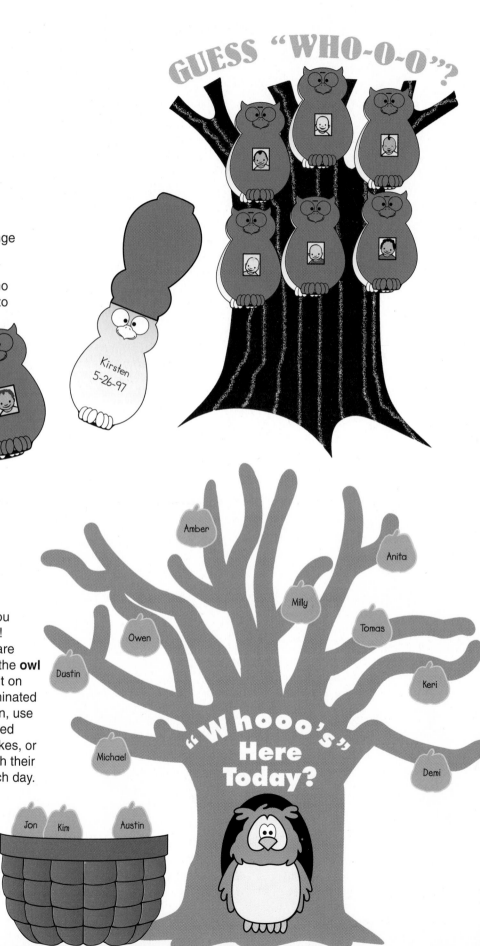

"Who-o-oo" can resist the cute baby faces in this display? Duplicate the **owl pattern** (page 90) onto brown paper and then onto white paper to make a class supply. Cut out the patterns. Staple one brown copy in front of a white copy along the tops. Glue a student's baby picture to the front of the pair; then label the inside with the child's name and birthdate. Arrange the owls on a paper tree so that they can be viewed easily. Encourage parents and children to look at each picture, guess who the child is, and then peek under the photo to find out!

Alesia Jewell—Preschool
Babes Welcome Place
Indianapolis, IN

This display lets everyone know that you really give a hoot who's present each day! Mount a paper tree so that the branches are within students' reach. Enlarge and color the **owl pattern** (page 91) character; then mount it on the tree along with a caption. Mount a laminated basket shape below the tree. Each season, use Sticky-Tac to attach personalized, laminated shapes—such as apples, leaves, snowflakes, or birds—to the basket. Ask children to attach their shapes to the branches as they arrive each day.

Karen Eiben—Three-Year-Olds
The Kids' Place
LaSalle, IL

# We're Falling For You!

Your classroom will glisten and glimmer with this unique fall tree. To begin, ask children to paint or color a large supply of cardboard tubes brown. Arrange the tubes on a wall to resemble a tree. Title the display as shown. Then invite each child to paint a sheet of paper with colored glitter glue. When the glue is dry, have her cut out a large leaf shape from the paper. Then use a permanent marker to write her name on the leaf. Tape the glittery leaves to the tree for a sparkling fall display! (Tip: Be sure to clean your paintbrushes well after this activity!)

Sheila Crawford—Five-Year-Olds
Kids Kampus
Huntington, IN

Judi Lesnansky
New Hope Academy
Youngstown, OH

Gather your youngsters to help you make this display. Mount a bulletin board–paper tree; then adorn it with students' sponge-painted leaf shapes. Have students glue orange and black tissue-paper pieces to paper plates to make a patch of jack-o'-lanterns; then pile the smiling pumpkins beneath the tree. You're really harvesting now!

Laura Fitz—Pre-K, Baltimore County Public School, Baltimore, MD

## "Orange" You Glad It's October?

If you'll be focusing on the color orange in October, use these ideas to make a bright fall display of students' projects. Cover your bulletin board with Halloween-themed fabric; then add an orange border and a title in orange letters. Use the display to show off any of the projects that students create during your orange studies, such as pumpkins and leaves.

Anita Edlund—Three-Year-Olds, Cokesbury Children's Center, Knoxville, TN

This colorful autumn display is sure to communicate your high expectations. Label several basket cutouts with classroom goals. Mount the baskets on a board along with a title and a tree cutout. Duplicate a supply of colorful **leaf patterns** (page 92). Personalize the leaves with students' names, and display them randomly on the tree's branches and across the board.

Elaine J. Swindell, Providence Preschool, Swan Quarter, NC

Mount a brown construction paper tree onto a wall. Attach a titled sign to the tree. Enlarge a set of **squirrel patterns** (page 93); then color and program them with the titles of your classroom jobs. Enlarge a classroom supply of **acorn patterns** (page 93); then color and program each with a different student's name. Mount the squirrels on and around the tree. Mount a student's acorn near each squirrel, replacing the acorns as new helpers are desired.

Wilma Droegemueller—Preschool and Gr. K
Zion Lutheran School
Mt. Pulaski, IL

To create the cornstalks for this display, roll up three or four pieces of green bulletin board paper and one piece of yellow bulletin board paper. Tape each roll to keep it from unraveling; then cut fringes in one end of each roll. Bend the fringes slightly. Slip the rolls inside one another, as shown, and staple them to a bulletin board. Add construction paper leaves to complete the cornstalks. Staple student-fingerpainted clouds and crows around the corn. Enlarge, color, and cut out a **scarecrow pattern** (page 94). Then add the scarecrow to this festive bulletin board.

Nancy O'Toole—Preschool, Ready Set Grow, Grand Rapids, MN

Welcome fall with this autumn garden. Cover your entrance with green and blue bulletin board paper and attach a white paper picket fence. To create a pumpkin, have each child sponge-paint a paper plate orange and glue on a construction paper stem and leaf. For sunflowers, have each child sponge-paint a small paper plate yellow and then glue sunflower seeds to the center and yellow construction paper rectangles around the outer edge. Mount the pumpkins and the sunflowers on your display. Then complete the effect with construction paper stems and leaves, curly ribbon vines, and a jolly scarecrow to welcome passersby.

adapted from an idea by Amy Wylie—Gr. K, Bluford Grade School, Bluford, IL

This progressive fall scene will keep onlookers checking back weekly to see what's new. To begin, enlist students' help to make a small scarecrow wearing sunglasses. Mount the scarecrow on a bulletin board and add the title "Fall Is Too Cool!" Each week, add students' fall craft projects—such as paper bag jack-o'-lanterns, sponge-painted leaves, or cardboard-tube bats—to create a new look. Finish the scene the last week of October by giving the scarecrow a trick-or-treat bag.

Pam Ingram—Gr. K, Davenport at School, Lenoir, NC

14

You're sure to get 101 compliments with this dalmatian display! Duplicate the **dog pattern** (page 95) onto white construction paper for each child. Have a child color the dog collar and nose, color and personalize the hat, and then press black fingerprints onto the dog. Cut out the pattern. Write a student-given name on the dog tag. In a word balloon, write a fire safety rule dictated by the child. Finally, display the dogs, the balloons, and a title on a bulletin board.

Lola M. Smith, Hilliard, OH

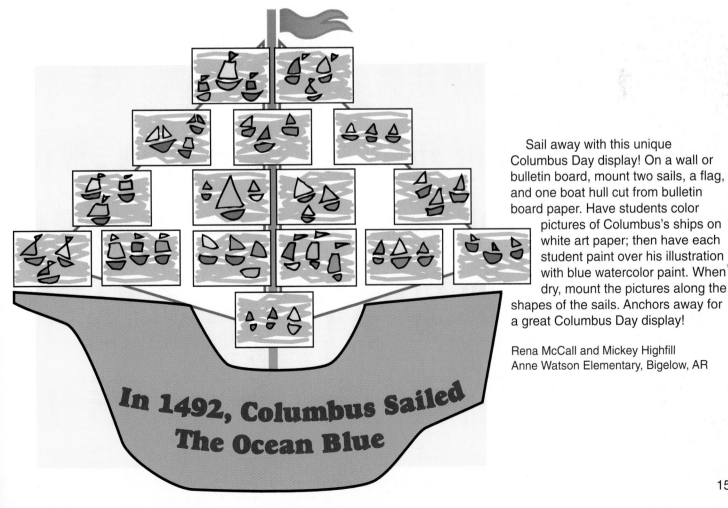

Sail away with this unique Columbus Day display! On a wall or bulletin board, mount two sails, a flag, and one boat hull cut from bulletin board paper. Have students color pictures of Columbus's ships on white art paper; then have each student paint over his illustration with blue watercolor paint. When dry, mount the pictures along the shapes of the sails. Anchors away for a great Columbus Day display!

Rena McCall and Mickey Highfill
Anne Watson Elementary, Bigelow, AR

How about a friendly scarecrow to encourage youngsters' counting skills? Stuff a set of children's clothes with newspaper to create a scarecrow; then display the fellow on a bulletin board along with a title. Invite each child to glue his choice of construction paper kernels onto a **corncob pattern** (page 95). For each child's ear of corn, personalize a tag and label it with the number of kernels. Add the corn and labels to the display. It might be corny, but it's learning that counts!

adapted from an idea by Eileen A. Saad—Pre-K, Meadowbrook Nursery School, Troy, MI

Spin a splendid display by stapling a yarn web onto a background. Then add spooky student-made spiders. To make one, glue together one large and one smaller paper circle. Add cutout eyes accented with black marker; then glue on accordion-folded paper legs.

Barbara Meyers, Fort Worth Country Day School, Fort Worth TX

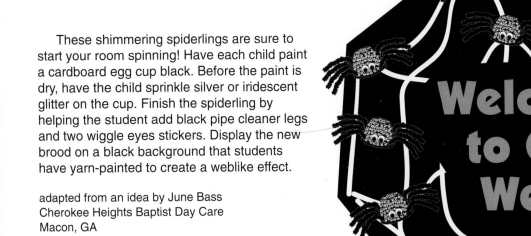

These shimmering spiderlings are sure to start your room spinning! Have each child paint a cardboard egg cup black. Before the paint is dry, have the child sprinkle silver or iridescent glitter on the cup. Finish the spiderling by helping the student add black pipe cleaner legs and two wiggle eyes stickers. Display the new brood on a black background that students have yarn-painted to create a weblike effect.

adapted from an idea by June Bass
Cherokee Heights Baptist Day Care
Macon, GA

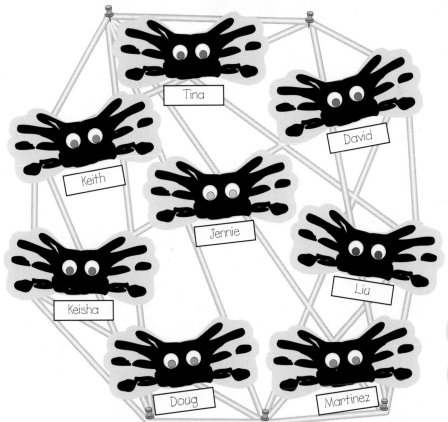

Feeling creepy? Use pushpins and glittery yarn to create a web on a wall. Then fill the web with a handful of spiders. To make a spider, direct a child to dip both hands into black paint and then press them onto paper. When the paint is dry, cut around the shape, removing the thumbprints. Glue on wiggle eyes stickers before adding the creepy-crawly and the child's name to the display.

Jennifer Liptak—Pre-K
Sonshine Preschool
Bensalem, PA

Looking for an easy Halloween art project? Have students cut out eyes, noses, mouths, ears, and other facial features from old magazines. Duplicate the **pumpkin pattern** (page 97) on orange paper for each child. After cutting out his pumpkin, the student glues facial features onto his cutout to create an out-of-the-ordinary pumpkin personality. Glue a small piece of sponge to the back of each pumpkin; then glue the sponge piece to the bulletin board to give a 3-D effect. There never was a pumpkin patch quite like this one!

Carve out some smiles with this interactive pumpkin display. Have each child create a jack-o'-lantern by gluing black construction paper shapes onto a **pumpkin pattern** (page 97) cutout. Program another pumpkin cutout as shown; then staple it over the child's jack-o'-lantern. Have the child glue a green construction paper stem onto the top pumpkin. Staple the pumpkins onto a bulletin board so they can be opened. Add twisted tissue paper vines and a title similar to the one shown. Come peek inside this pumpkin patch!

adapted from an idea by Sarah Booth—PreK, Messiah Nursery School, South Williamsport, PA

"Whoooo" lurks within? Let's see! Photocopy the **haunted house pattern** (page 98) on construction paper. (Make enough copies so that you'll have one window or door for each child in your class.) Have children color the houses; then cut slits along the dotted lines. Tape a different child's photo behind each door or window. Display the houses among craft spiderwebbing and a title. Encourage children to go haunting around, looking for each other in this display.

Dana Vitole—Gr. K
Blessed Sacrament School
Paterson, NJ

Here's a "spook-tacular" display for October. Loosely staple a large ghost cutout on a bulletin board, leaving a small section unstapled. Stuff the ghost with plastic grocery bags; then finish stapling it. Next mount a photo of each child as an infant or a toddler to a **child pattern** (page 128). Tape only the top edge of a sheet of paper labeled "Guess Who?" over each picture. Mount each child cutout around the ghost. Can *you* guess who?

Barbara Meyers—Gr. K, Fort Worth Country Day School, Fort Worth, TX

This seasonal display is a real treat! Have each child paint an orange stripe and yellow stripe across a **candy corn pattern** (page 99). When the paint is dry, help each child cut out her candy corn. Then label the candy corn with the children's names. Display these child-made treats on a bulletin board and then add a title.

Sarah Booth—Four- and Five-Year-Olds
Messiah Nursery School
South Williamsport, PA

Get everyone's hands in on this great gobbler! Cut two paper grocery bags so that they open flat; then crumple the bags in water. When dry, mount the bags on the board and stuff with newspaper. Add head and leg cutouts to the turkey body. Have each child select a color of paint and then make handprints on a separate, large sheet of white art paper. After folding back the sides of the dried projects, staple them around the turkey's body to resemble feathers.

Beth Crawford and Barb Willis
John Celine School
Decorah, IA

This display of plump little turkeys is perfect for the Thanksgiving holiday. To make one turkey, trace a child's hand onto a sheet of fall-colored construction paper. Place four different-colored sheets of paper under the tracing; then cut through all thicknesses of paper to create five hand shapes. Have the child glue the shapes onto a turkey body cutout to resemble feathers and then add paper features. Display the turkeys on a picket fence made from bulletin board paper. Gobble! Gobble!

Kacie Farmer—Five-Year-Olds, Welborn Children's Center, Evansville, IN

Forget the dinner table. This gorgeous gobbler's place is in the hall for all to admire! Mount a large turkey body cutout on a wall. Cut a class supply of paper strips from bulletin board paper and obtain several sea sponges and/or handled dishwashing sponges. Have each child use one of the sponges to paint his strip in a color of his preference. After the paint dries, attach the strips behind the turkey to create some flashy tail feathers. Happy Thanksgiving!

If your children like making paper chains and fingerpainting, then they're sure to enjoy this turkey display that improves finger dexterity! To create the turkey's body, ask your children to help you make a paper chain of brown construction paper strips. Staple the chain in a spiral fashion to a background. Attach a paper head and neck to the center of the circle and paper legs below the chain. Top the turkey off with colorful feathers cut from fingerpainted paper.

Jane FitzSimmons-Thomez—Preschool
St. Mary's School
Owatonna, MN

# Turkey Dressing

These tricky turkeys will tickle your students' imaginations! For each child, duplicate the **turkey pattern** (page 100) on tagboard. Have each child team up with his family (at home) to disguise his turkey in hopes of avoiding the turkey's Thanksgiving Day demise. Display each completed turkey; then invite children to guess the identity of each turkey-disguise designer.

Lisa Lucas—Gr. K
Saints Peter and Paul School
Garfield Heights, OH

Let this turkey talk your students into being on their best behavior during November! Enlarge the **turkey pattern** (page 101). Color and cut out the turkey; then mount it on the board with the poem. Cut out and display enlarged paper **feather patterns** (page 101) in a pocket as shown. Each time good behavior is exhibited by the entire class, staple a feather to the turkey. When all of the feathers have been added to ol' Tom, treat students to a popcorn party!

These wise owls seem to know what's important in life! Give each child an **owl pattern** (page 102). Provide construction paper scraps, scissors, glue, and markers. Encourage each child to create an original owl. Mount each child's owl on the board along with a speech bubble containing that child's thankful thoughts for the holiday season.

Johanna Jansen—Gr. K, St. Agatha School, Portland, OR

23

Everyone's thankful about this bulletin board! Arrange brown (land), light blue (sky), and dark blue (water) background paper as shown. Next, cut out a large ship and staple it in the water. Invite each child to color and cut out a copy of one of the **people patterns** (page 103). Glue a photo of the child's face to his cutout. Then add the personalized Pilgrims and Native Americans to the board along with hearts containing children's writing or dictation.

adapted from ideas by
Denise Lindsay—Gr. K, Hampton Bays Elementary, Hampton Bays, NY
Ann Schmidt—Gr. K, Lafayette Christian School, Lafayette, IN
Laura Cozzi and Kim McAlpine—Gr. K, Truman School, Parlin, NJ

If you study Native American tribes in November, you'll want to create this terrific totem pole display! Have each student paint a brown paper grocery bag to resemble a bird or an animal. Later, have him fill his bag with crumpled newspaper and then add construction paper features such as a beak and wings. Using staples or duct tape, stack and mount the bags onto a wall or a large bulletin board. After explaining that totem poles were used for storytelling, challenge youngsters to create tall tales their totem poles might share.

Barbara Meyers
Fort Worth Country Day
Fort Worth, TX

# Winter

The weather outside may be frightful, but this board is truly delightful! Have each student glue two white paper doilies on a sheet of blue construction paper to create a snowman. Then have her embellish her snowy friend with craft items. Set out white paint and cotton swabs, and encourage students to dab paint around their snowmen to create snow. And for an extra special touch, tape a string of white Christmas tree lights around the bulletin board.

Kiva English—Gr. K, Cato-Meridian School, Cato, NY, and Tara Kicklighter—Grs. K–1, Bunnell Elementary School, Bunnell, FL

Warm up to winter's chill with this friendly bulletin board. Enlarge the **mittens pattern** (page 104) on bulletin board paper. Cut out the mittens and then staple them to a bulletin board. Help each youngster fold and then cut out her own snowflake shape from white paper. Glue the child's photo to the center of her snowflake; then add the snowflake to the board. Finish by writing the title on the mittens as shown.

26    Elinor Gesink—Gr. K, Sheldon Christian School, Sheldon, IA

Brrr! This wintry bulletin board will get flurries of attention! Provide each student with construction paper, scissors, glue, two craft sticks, and a penguin pattern if desired. Have each child trace or draw a penguin and then cut on the resulting outline. Have him glue craft sticks on the penguin to represent skis. Mount the penguins on a dark blue background along with cotton-batting snowdrifts and snowflake cutouts. Let it snow!

Carol Denny—Three- and Four-Year-Olds, First Baptist Church, Conyers, GA

Recognize and appreciate the diversity among children with this wintry flurry! Give each child a square piece of white paper; then demonstrate ways that he can repeatedly fold it. Have the child make snips and cuts through the folded paper, being sure to leave some of the folded edges intact. Then have him glue his photo to the opened snowflake. Mount each snowflake on the board with the title as shown.

Laura Cozzi—Gr. K, Truman Elementary School, Parlin, NJ

To make this wintry scene, encourage a flurry of activity several days in advance. During center times, have students stamp or stencil background paper with snowflake designs, make white paper chains, and trace and cut out green hand outlines. When the background is in place, staple the hand cutouts to the board to form a tree. Curl the fingertips of the cutouts by wrapping them around a pencil. Staple cotton batting to the board for accumulated snow. As the finishing touch, staple the paper chains to the board to form a snowman's body; then attach stick arms and a real scarf, hat, and mittens. Brrrr! It's cold in here!

Christine Hammerschmidt—Gr. K Special Education, Hillcrest School, Morristown, NJ

To create this display, have each child use paint to make a white footprint on a dark blue sheet of construction paper. When the paint is dry, cut out the footprint and then help the child use a permanent marker to draw eyes and a mouth on it. Next, have him glue on construction paper arms, a nose, and a scarf. Display these frosty friends on a wall or bulletin board with paper snowdrifts and cutout snowflakes.

Shelley Williams—Three- and Four-Year-Olds
Children's College
Layton, UT

Using white chalk and assorted crayons, have each student draw a winter scene on a piece of light blue construction paper. Then have her dictate a corresponding story. Mount the projects on a dark blue background, along with snowflake cutouts and a title. Staple lengths of curled curling ribbon to the board. Then hang several snowflakes from the ceiling in front of the board. Let it snow! Let it snow! Let it snow!

Kathleen Sherbon—Gr. K, North County Christian School, Paso Robles, CA

Snoozing, student-made bears are the subject of this wintry bulletin board. To create a hibernating hideout for bear art projects, mount a cave and tree cutout onto a blue background. Glue cotton batting over the cave and the branches of the tree. Mount wallpaper clouds and snowflake cutouts, along with a friendly sign, to add the finishing touches to this wintry scene.

Nancy Barad and Rona Cohen, Bet Yeladim Preschool, Columbia, MD

# Peace On Earth Begins With Me!

When your students contribute to this display, entire families can take pride in its important message. Using the **doll pattern** (page 105), make enlarged photocopies on multicultural colors of construction paper. Ask each child to choose a doll cutout, then work with his family members to decorate his doll to represent his heritage. Provide adult assistance at school for those who need it. Then enlarge the **Earth pattern** (page 105) onto blue bulletin-board paper and cut it out. Have children sponge-paint the continents. Display the Earth, dolls, and title as shown. Encourage children to talk about their dolls and their heritages.

Mimi Duffy—Gr. K
Memorial School
Paramus, NJ

Invite each child to make an angel for this display. To make one, cut a nine-inch paper plate into four wedge-shaped pieces. Glue together three of the pieces to make the angel's body. To make the angel's arm, cut the fluted border off the fourth piece and then glue the border to the body. Glue a paper circle to the body. Draw facial features on the circle. Staple a length of garland to the head to create a halo; then glue on yarn or raffia for hair. Mount each angel beside a photograph of the child who created it. How heavenly!

Nancy O'Toole—Preschool
Ready, Set, Grow
Grand Rapids, MN

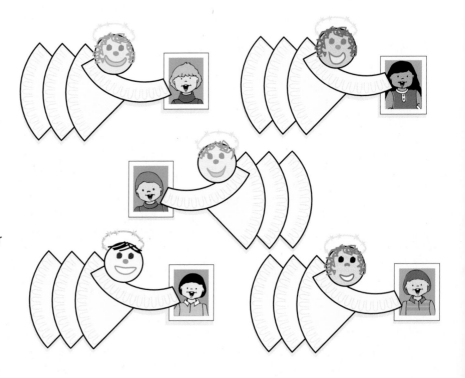

No matter which holidays youngsters celebrate, everyone makes a glowing contribution to this board. In advance use the **candlestick-holder pattern** (page 106) to make several tracers. Then have each child paint a paper-towel tube silver or gold. Next have him trace and cut out a candlestick holder, then decorate it using paper scraps and glitter glue. Have the child stuff a tissue-paper flame in the top of his dry candle and then write his name on the board. Staple each candle and holder on the titled board.

Vivian Campbell—Gr. K, Knollwood School, Piscataway, NJ

Display your students' good work in holiday style! Staple a holiday garland around a colorful background. Cut out the title's letters from wrapping paper; then mount them on the board. When a child completes a piece of work that he is particularly proud of, invite him to mount it on the board and add a gift bow. What a pretty sight!

Monica Marino—Special Education, Shady Lane School, Deptford Township, NJ

31

# Lights Are Shining Ever Bright!

Brighten your classroom with this dazzling display! Cut sponges into narrow rectangular shapes. Have each child sponge-paint a menorah, a kinara, or other candle shapes onto white construction paper. When the paint is dry, glue on scrunched-up tissue-paper flames. Mount each picture on a slightly larger sheet of colorful construction paper; then arrange the pictures on a board with a border and a caption.

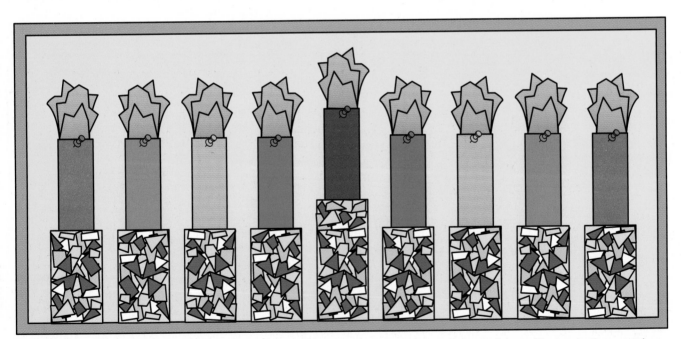

Each of the candles on this menorah will sparkle and glow as you go through the holidays. To create the mosaic-style menorah, have students glue paper pieces onto nine large bulletin board paper rectangles. Mount the pieces on a background. Next, cut out nine more bulletin board paper rectangles to represent the candles. Mount the shammash (central candle) and "light" it with a tissue paper flame. Each day, have students help you add another candle and flame to celebrate. Adapt this idea to celebrate Kwanzaa by creating seven rectangular paper candle holders. Then add three red, one black, and three green construction paper candles. Each day "light" one candle by adding one tissue paper flame.

Nancy Goldberg—Three-Year-Olds, B'nai Israel Schilit Nursery School, Rockville, MD

Looking for an "a-door-able" holiday display? Try this! Mount a large cookie jar cutout on your classroom door; then have each child decorate a **gingerbread cookie pattern** (page 107). Mount the projects as shown. How sweet it is!

This display helps youngsters understand that the most special gifts are gifts they give of themselves. Have each child write (or dictate for you to write) about something that he could do over the holidays to help or care for someone else. Mount the writings on foil wrapping paper. Give each child a bow to stick onto his project.

Traci Schaffert
Hillcrest School
Morristown, NJ

I will walk my dog.

Jeremy

I can put away my shoes.

Amy

I will play with my brother.

Becky

I will ask my friend to go to the movies.

Keisha

I will watch my baby sister.

Kirk

I can help Grandma reach things.

Clevell

I will sort the socks for Mom.

Nick

I can take out the trash.

Holly

To make this terrific tree display, copy and cut out a **yellow star pattern** (page 108) for each child. Then glue the child's photo to the center of the star. Mount the stars in rows to form triangular tree shapes; then staple a construction paper trunk to the bottom of each tree. If desired, add a string of holiday lights around the border of the display. Plug the lights into a nearby outlet and watch your students' faces light up!

Bonnie Martin—Preschool, Hopewell Country Day School, Pennington, NJ

Deck the halls and walls with this display that counts down the days until Christmas! Staple a Christmas tree cutout to a bulletin board. Then add 25 student-decorated gift box cutouts that open with brads. Label each box with a different number from 1 to 25. Place an ornament cutout inside each box and close the lid. On the first day of December, open the box labeled with the numeral 1, remove the ornament, and then use a pushpin to attach it to the tree. After counting down each of the days in this manner, the tree will be completely decorated and ready for Santa by Christmas!

Pam Vannatta—Four-Year-Olds, Kids N Kapers Nursery School, Lexington, KY

Snuggle down into making this display for the cozy winter holidays. For each child, copy the **headboard** and **footboard patterns** (page 109) on brown construction paper. Have each child cut out a pillowcase, sized to fit the patterns. Then have her glue her photo (or draw a self-portrait) on the pillowcase. Have her use fabric scraps to create a quilt, also sized to fit the bed. Then have her glue the pieces together. Make a cozy door display by mounting each child's project on a large wreath or quilt.

Patricia A. Locke
Canal Winchester, OH

To create this dreamy scene, cut out a large headboard shape and mount it on a board. Add stuffed paper pillows. Have each child use various art supplies to decorate a construction-paper square. Attach each child's square to a construction-paper blanket to resemble a quilt. Staple the quilt loosely to the board. Have each child make a paper-plate face; then mount the plates above the quilt. Sweet dreams!

Sheli Gossett—Gr. K, Sebring, FL

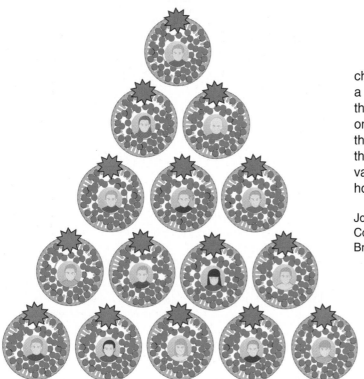

This display doubles as a great gift idea. Invite each child to use red and green ink-filled bingo markers to paint a white paper plate. Take a picture of each child; then trim the developed photos into circles. Glue each child's photo onto the center of his plate. Punch a hole near the top of the plate; then attach lengths of curling ribbon. Arrange the plates in a tree shape on a wall. Just before Christmas vacation, remove the plates from the wall, and send them home to parents.

Joan Johnson—Four-Year-Olds
Columbus School
Bridgeport, CT

These merry little elves are quite a project, but the results are worth it! To make one, have a child lie on white bulletin board paper in a pose of his choice. Trace around his body and then cut out the figure. Use a digital camera to take the child's photo. Then load the photo on a computer, enlarge the child's face, and print it out. (You can also use an actual photo and a copier.) Have the child use paints and construction paper to make his elf clothing and shoes. Finally, attach the child's face to his figure. Mount these holiday elves down your hallway for a dazzling display!

Angelena Pritchard—Gr. K,
Fountain Inn Elementary
Fountain Inn, SC

Santa Claus is coming to town and to your classroom! First determine the width that you'd like your display to be. Then cut two sheets of red bulletin board paper accordingly. Also cut an equal length of tan and white bulletin board paper. Trim a scalloped border around the white sheet to resemble Santa's beard. Glue the beard to the bottom of the tan sheet (the face). Then trim one of the red sheets to resemble Santa's hat. Glue the hat to the top of the face. Use construction paper scraps, along with cotton balls or fiberfill, to create details for Santa's hat and face. Finally, glue the remaining red sheet of paper below the beard to resemble Santa's body. If desired, add black construction paper legs to complete this jolly old elf. Display your students' holiday-related work on Santa's spacious belly.

Michelle Wilson—Gr. K
Park Springs Elementary School
Coral Springs, FL

Adorn your classroom wall or door with this angelic display. Cut out a large construction paper wreath. Mount the wreath, and add construction paper holly leaves and a bow. For each child, copy an **angel pattern** (page 110) on sturdy, white paper. Have each child glue a photo of his face on the angel and then decorate his angel using gold and silver crayons, paint pens, pasta, and glitter. Mount each angel on the wreath; then add the title.

adapted from an idea
by Carolyn Johnson—Gr. K
W. A. Carpenter Elementary, Deer Park, TX

37

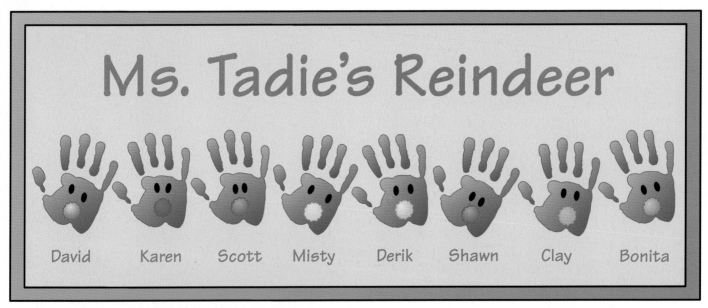

# Ms. Tadie's Reindeer

David   Karen   Scott   Misty   Derik   Shawn   Clay   Bonita

This row of reindeer will add some holiday charm to a hallway or your classroom! Paint each child's palm and fingers with brown tempera paint. Have the child press his hand onto a long sheet of bulletin board paper; then write his name under the resulting print. Have students make a row of handprints on the paper. When the prints are dry, invite each child to add construction paper eyes and a pom-pom nose to his print. Label the display to resemble the one shown, and you're ready for a sleigh ride!

Robin Tadie—Preschool, Audubon School, Colorado Springs, CO

**Countdown!**

Let's count the days
'til Christmas
In an extra special way
And take a bell off Rudolph;
One bell every day.
Rudolph is our helper
And if we watch,
we'll see
When Christmas is upon us
With fun for you and me!

Rudolph is ready to help your youngsters count—backwards! Mount a large **reindeer pattern** (page 111) along with a copy of the poem (shown) onto a bulletin board. Use Sticky-Tac to attach the same number of large jingle bells onto the collar of the reindeer as there are days until the holiday. Surround Rudolph with your students' various holiday projects. Remove a bell each day and count down together. With this great display, you'll go down in history!

Debbie Korytoski—Gr. K, Pine Ridge Elementary, Ellerslie, GA

Recognize the new year by making festive party hats and declaring resolutions! Have children use art supplies—such as glitter paint, gift-wrap scraps, tinsel, and tissue paper—to decorate **hat patterns** (page112). Mount each hat on a board with a title. Record each child's resolution on a **paper strip pattern** (page 112) below his hat. Happy New Year, everybody!

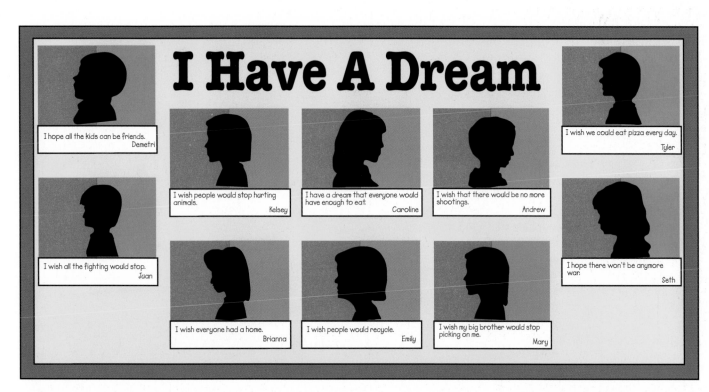

After discussing Martin Luther King Jr., this bulletin board is a natural follow-up. Using an overhead projector, outline each child's profile on black construction paper and cut it out. For each child, tape a red and a green sheet of construction paper side by side; then mount his profile in the center. Give each child a 3" x 18" strip of paper on which to write (or dictate) his own dream for the world. Display each mounted profile with that child's written dream.

Adapted from an idea by Tracey Gest—Gr. K, Houston Elementary, Austin, TX

Your study of Washington and Lincoln can be a springboard to instill career ambitions in your students. Enlarge and photocopy the **president patterns** (page 113) on construction paper. Cut out the presidential silhouettes; then mount them on a board along with each child's silhouette. Have each child illustrate his current aspirations for his future. Then mount each illustration under the corresponding child's silhouette.

Bobbie Hallman, Burbank School, Merced, CA

How do you say "I love you" without saying a word? With sign language, of course! Teach your youngsters the hand sign for "I love you." Then decorate your classroom for Valentine's Day with this "hand-some" display. First, have a student place her hand on an overhead projector. Trace the enlarged image onto bulletin board paper; then cut it out. Fold the middle and ring fingers down and glue them to the palm. Attach the hand cutout to a wall with the title "I Love You!" Encourage each child to illustrate something or someone she loves; then display these pictures around the cutout. Love is in the air!

Pat Murray—Gr. K
St. Rita of Cascia School
Aurora, IL

Love will be in the air with this eye-catching display! Have each child cover a heart cutout with red and pink tissue paper squares. Glue a small photo of the child to the middle of the heart. Have the child glue the heart to the inside of an open envelope and then write her name on the outside as shown. Mount a large **mailbox pattern** (page 114) cutout on a wall or bulletin board. Display the child-made valentines so they appear to be coming out of the mailbox. Will you be mine?

Cathy McCain—Two-Year-Olds, Peachtree Corners Baptist Preschool, Norcross, GA

These valentines make the perfect matches! Sponge-paint a different letter on each of a supply of construction paper hearts. Arrange these hearts on a board along with the title. Then glue pictures that begin with those chosen letters on smaller heart cutouts. To make the border, have each child sponge-paint his initials on a strip of art paper. Encourage students to match each picture to its correct beginning sound.

Ricke Bly—Gr. K, RTR Elementary, Ruthton, MN

Here's the perfect February match for reading skills. Have each child trace and cut out one white heart and one pink heart. Write each child's name on the top of his white heart; then mount it on the board. Have the child glue his photo to the pink heart and then decorate the heart with art supplies. Use Sticky-Tac to mount the decorated hearts along the bottom of the board. Then invite children to match the photos to the names.

Nan Hokanson—Four- and Five-Year-Olds, Circle Time Preschool, Sheboygan Falls, WI

Have your sweet ones help you make this valentine display. Enlarge, color, and cut out the **cat pattern** (page 115). Then create a wagon as shown. To fill the wagon, have youngsters paint candy-kiss shapes brown and then wrap the candies in foil. Label each kiss with a personalized tag. Border your display with pink handprints on white paper circles that have been mounted on red and pink hearts.

Diane Guffey—Three-Year-Olds, ABC Learning Center, Rockport, TX

# Spring & Summer

Highlight your precious little ones in this sparkling display. Enlarge and duplicate the **leprechaun** and **pot patterns** (page 116). Color and cut out the patterns; then mount them on a bulletin board. Have each child cut out a large, gold construction paper coin and then glue his picture on it. After each child decorates his coin with glitter, mount each coin above the pot. Use glitter glue to write a seasonal message.

Beverly Brown—Grs. K–4
Ninety Six Elementary
Ninety Six, SC

Incite creative "green-making" with this seasonal project. For each child, copy the **shamrock pattern** (page 115) on white construction paper. Encourage children to think of creative ways to make their shamrocks green. You might get the wheels turning by suggesting blue and yellow paints, a magazine color search, or a collage of fabrics. Have each child cut out her finished project and then staple it to the board. If desired, attach a stuffed green frog and a caption.

Adapted from an idea by AnnaLisa R. Damminger—Gr. K, West Jersey Child Development Center, Voorhees, NJ

Let this flock of feathered friends boost self-esteem! Enlarge the **duck character pattern** (page 117); color, laminate, and cut it out before posting it on the board. Add a few cut-out raindrops to the display. Duplicate a **duck pattern** (page 117) on yellow paper for each child. Each Monday use a wipe-off marker to write a child's name on the umbrella. Have students label their duck cutouts with positive comments about the honored child. Wipe the umbrella clean at the end of the week, duplicate more ducks, and you'll be ready for Monday!

This adaptable board provides each child with her own display space. Cut out a large construction paper circle for each child, plus one extra. Decorate the extra circle to resemble a caterpillar's head. For each child, duplicate a pair of construction paper **sneaker patterns** (page 118). Have each child color and cut out her sneakers and then glue construction paper legs and sneakers to her personalized caterpillar body part. Mount the body parts behind the caterpillar head, going as far around your room as necessary. Use each body part to display that student's choice of work. (Adapt the title to coincide with your studies by replacing *Spring* with other topics, such as *Summer, Books, Manners, Science,* etc.)

Pamela Buettner—Gr. K, Belleville, IL

## Our Classroom Bouquet

Each child contributes to this giant display in a big way! Precut a circle in the center of a paper plate for each child; then personalize the plate. Have each child glue paper petals, a stem, and leaves to the plate. Tape the child's picture to the back of the plate. Arrange the flowers on a wall along with a paper pot. Add a class photo to the pot and a title to the display.

Theresa Reth—Four-Year-Olds, Little People's College, New Bedford, MA

Use self-adhesive letters to label a large **watering can pattern** (page 119) with your school's name. Collect artificial flowers; then label each flower with a different child's name by attaching a personalized construction paper circle to its center. Mount the watering can, flowers, a sun cutout, and crumpled tissue paper grass on a blue background. Complete the board by mounting a title and a sprinkling of raindrops labeled with your daily activities or learning goals.

Linda Madden and Kerri Madden Curtis—Pre-K, Sacred Heart School, Crosby, TX

Here's colorful proof positive that your students are growing! Mount brown ground strips along a background. Then have each child make prints from the following growing parts of her body: hands (flower petals), forearm (stem), and feet (leaves). Cut out and assemble the parts. Glue seeds to the center of the petals; then mount each flower. For roots, have each child staple on several pieces of yarn the length of her fingers.

Erin K. Lom—Gr. K, Tiffany Creek Elementary, Boyceville, WI

Here's a soft touch of spring. To make lambs, cut out large, black cloudlike shapes, and have student pairs use white paint to sponge-paint them. Mount the shapes on the board; then add construction paper faces, ears, and feet. Have each child use colorful art materials to make a flower. Glue each child's photo to the center of his flower. Mount the flowers among construction paper and tissue paper grass.

Diane Bonica, Tigard-Tualatin School District, Tualatin, OR

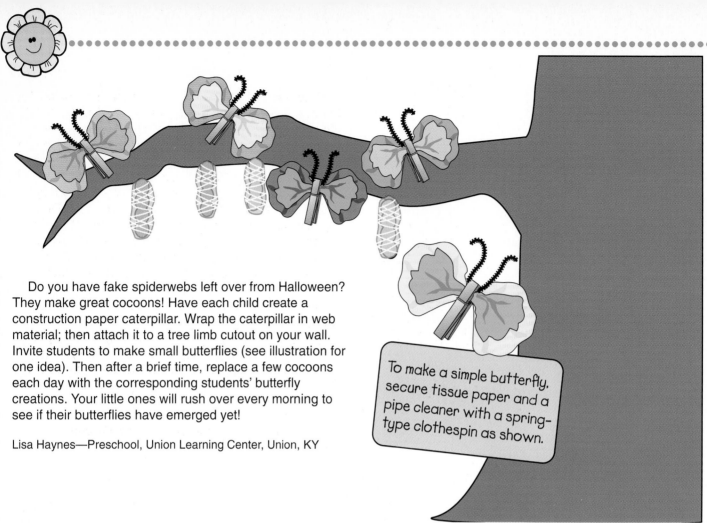

Do you have fake spiderwebs left over from Halloween? They make great cocoons! Have each child create a construction paper caterpillar. Wrap the caterpillar in web material; then attach it to a tree limb cutout on your wall. Invite students to make small butterflies (see illustration for one idea). Then after a brief time, replace a few cocoons each day with the corresponding students' butterfly creations. Your little ones will rush over every morning to see if their butterflies have emerged yet!

Lisa Haynes—Preschool, Union Learning Center, Union, KY

To make a simple butterfly, secure tissue paper and a pipe cleaner with a spring-type clothespin as shown.

To create this display, cover the bottom half of a blue background with white paper. Sponge-paint the white paper brown to resemble dirt; then use your finger to draw worm tunnels in the wet paint. Mount paper grass above the dirt. Have each child make a worm by sliding Cheerios cereal pieces onto a pipe cleaner and then bending each end to hold the cereal in place. Mount the worms on the board and add cutout butterflies and flowers as desired.

Pam Ingram and Sandy Ingram—Gr. K, Davenport School, Lenoir, NC

# "Bee" A Reader!

Even reluctant readers will be motivated to contribute to this honey of a display! In advance, duplicate a supply of the **honeycomb pattern** (page 120) on yellow construction paper. Also keep a large box of Honeycomb cereal on hand. To make a large bee, cut out the simple shapes of the bee (see the illustration) from tagboard. Cover the abdomen and head with black construction paper. Cover the middle section with yellow fake fur or felt. Also cut out and glue on stripes from the same yellow fabric. Cover each eye circle with green foil paper; then add a smaller black construction paper circle to each center. Attach curled pipe cleaners to resemble antennae. Finally, cover the wing shapes with waxed paper; then glue all of the parts together. Post the bee along with a title and some colorful tissue paper flowers. When each child has read (or listened to) a book, give him a section of honeycomb. Have him write the title of his book and add an illustration. Each time a child adds a section to the honeycomb, invite him to scoop out a handful of cereal for a job well done!

adapted from an idea by Betty Kobes, West Hancock Elementary School

This board's designed for versatility! Mount yellow copies of the **beehive pattern** (page 121) on a board. Label each hive with the skill(s) of your choice (such as vowels, as shown). Have children use art supplies to make bees. Ask children to cut out pictures that have a beginning or middle vowel sound; then glue them to their bees. Store the bees in a bag. To use the board, have a child use Sticky-Tac to mount the bees on the appropriate hotel.

Adapted from an idea by Barbara Pasley, Energy Elementary, Energy, IL

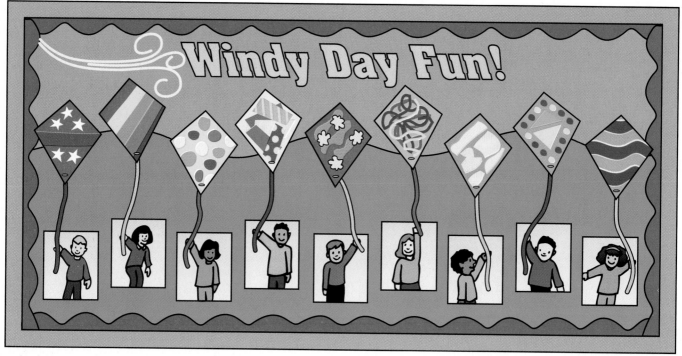

Let's go fly a kite! In advance, take a photo of each child posing as if she were flying a kite. Mount each photo on a background as shown. Invite each child to use art supplies to decorate a **kite pattern** (page 122). Then help her staple a length of yarn to the back of the kite. Glue the loose end of the yarn to the child's photo; then staple the kite to the board. Whoosh—off it goes!

Leah Taylor—Gr. K, Maranatha Chapel, San Diego, CA

It's true! April showers really do bring flowers. And my, aren't these May blooms creative? To make an umbrella, a child glues portions of the weather section of the newspaper onto a piece of construction paper. He then traces an enlarged **umbrella pattern** (page 122) and cuts out the shape. Alongside the umbrellas, display flowers that students create from their choice of papers and a variety of craft supplies.

Lynn Anderson and Lauren Ingle, Friendship Connection, Maplewood, MN

# A Few Of Our Favorite Things

These are a few of your favorite things! After sharing "My Favorite Things" from a soundtrack of *The Sound of Music,* have each child illustrate one of his favorite things on a **raindrop pattern** (page 123). Then have the child cut out his raindrop. To create a slick, rainy effect, cover each child's raindrop with clear plastic wrap before mounting it on the board with a title and a border of paper roses.

Susan Brown—Gr. K, Southside Elementary, Tuscumbia, AL

Plip, plop—here come the raindrops! Mount a storm cloud cutout above an outdoor scene. Invite your youngsters to cut raindrops from metallic paper (or aluminum foil). Staple the rain to the board. Then help each child dip his hand in brown tempera paint and make a handprint near the bottom of the board as shown. Oh, lovely mud!

Leah Treen and Chris Lewis—Four-Year-Olds, Hillwood Baptist Preschool, Huntsville, AL

# "CHICK" IT OUT!

**Spring Picnic**

**This Week!**

**Help Needed:**

Use this clever display to get parents to take a peek at your current classroom events. At one end of a hallway, mount two halves of a large, cracked poster board egg; then fill the remaining hall space with chick projects. To make each chick, use brads to attach a student's cutout hand shapes to a copy of the **egg pattern** (page 123); then add paper feet, eyes, and a beak along with feathers, if desired. Add to the display current announcements or pictures of your spring activities.

Help each child use different colors of bingo markers to create a pattern on a copy of the **egg pattern** (page 123). Next, fringe one side of a length of green bulletin board paper to resemble grass. Staple the length on a display to create a pocket. Add more grass pockets, if desired. Tuck the decorated eggs in the grass; then put a real basket near the display. To use, a child takes an egg out of the grass. He then identifies the pattern before putting the egg in the basket.

adapted from an idea by Betsy Ruggiano—Preschool
Featherbed Lane School
Clark, NJ

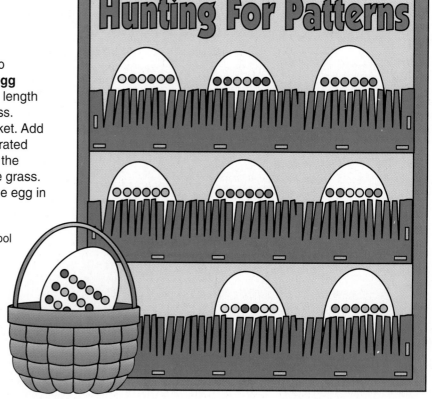

Hunting For Patterns

Enlarge the **bunny pattern** (page 124) several times. Color each bunny, creating a unique design on each bow tie and leaving the eggs white. For each bunny, cut four construction paper eggs that correspond in size to the eggs in the basket. Color each set of four eggs to match a bunny's bow tie. Laminate the bunnies and eggs. Attach the loop sides of Velcro pieces to the backs of the eggs, and attach the hook sides of Velcro pieces to the eggs in the baskets. Mount the bunnies on a background, and store the eggs in a real basket. To manipulate the display, a child attaches the corresponding eggs to each bunny's basket.

Donna Austin, St. Matthew's Preschool, Lehighton, PA

Cover a board with a lightly patterned pastel fabric. Use an opaque projector to enlarge the **bunny pattern** (page 125). Using a black marker, trace the pattern onto white poster board. Color in the pink parts as shown. Mount the bunny on the board; then add the title and fringe-cut construction paper grass. After studying various types of decorated eggs, have each child design and paint a very large egg to add to the display.

Teresa Hatton—Gr. K, Hutchison Beach Elementary, Panama City Beach, FL

Need a handsome door display? Cut a large basket shape from bulletin board paper; then have youngsters paint handprints on the basket to give it texture. Trace one of each child's hands onto construction paper. Personalize the hand shapes; then cut them out. Mount the basket on your door; then arrange the hands over it to form a handle. Secure a real bow to the door. Fill the basket with snazzy student-decorated eggs.

Carolyn M. Patterson—Preschool, Grove City
Head Start, Grove City, PA

Hippity hoppity! Here comes the Easter Bunny with some "eggs-tra" nice eggs. Enlarge, color and cut out the **bunny pattern** (page 126); then mount it on a background. Have each child use watercolor paints to paint a large, construction paper egg shape. When the paint is dry, cut a circle from the center of each child's egg; then tape a picture of the child to the back. Add the eggs, a border of fringed-paper grass, and a title to your seasonal display.

Barb Johnson and Dona Peck—Preschool, ECSE Preschool, John Cline Elementary, Decorah, IA

# Celebrate The Young Child !

Promote the Week of the Young Child with this child-made display. Provide each child with a skin-toned construction paper **doll pattern** (page 127) to decorate with a variety of materials, such as wallpaper, feathers, fabric, yarn, sequins, lace, and markers. Mount each child's project on a personalized piece of construction paper. Display these projects at a location in your community, such as the library, a grocery store, or a school administration building.

Roxanne Rowley—Early Childhood Specialist, Four Stars Preschool, Manistee, MI

Celebrate the star qualities of every child with this display. Take a picture of each child standing in the position shown (arms straight out at shoulder height and legs apart). From each developed photo, cut out a star shape around the child's body. Mount the photo onto a piece of paper; then trim a larger star shape around the photo. Arrange the photos on a display along with star shapes that have been student decorated with glitter and other shiny materials. Brilliant!

adapted from an idea by Sheri Dressler—PreK
Woodland School
Carpentersville, IL

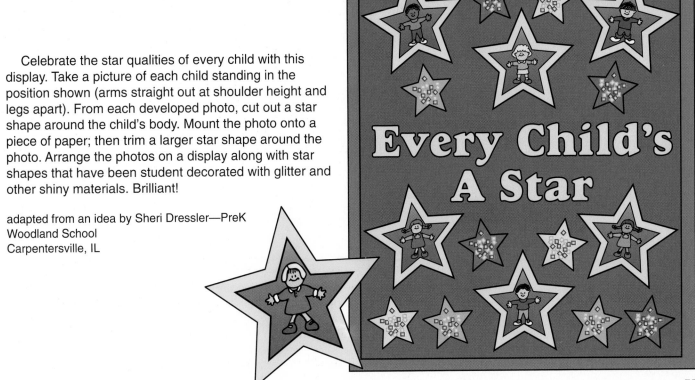

# The Whole World's In Our Hands

Recognize Earth Day with this display. Enlarge the **earth pattern** (page 105) and cut it out. Have youngsters twist green and blue pieces of tissue paper, then glue them onto the pattern. Enlarge the **child pattern** (page 105). For each child, duplicate the pattern onto skin-toned construction paper; then cut it out. Ask each child to decorate his pattern using various art supplies so that it resembles himself. Mount the earth and student projects on a background, adding a title if desired.

Jean Jaffe and Sandra Wright—Preschool
Copeland Run Learning Center
Downingtown, PA

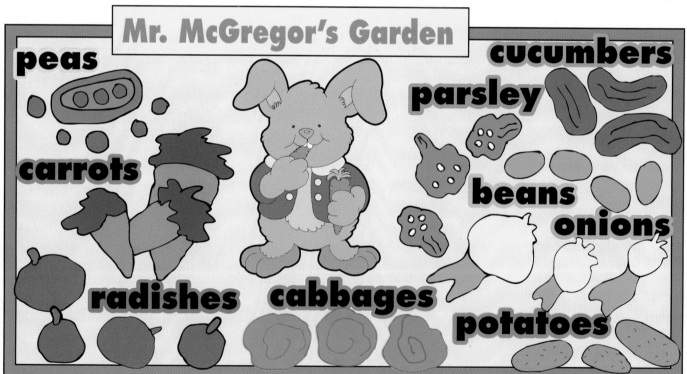

If you're studying rabbits, gardens, vegetables, or nutrition—this board's for you! Enlarge and duplicate the **rabbit pattern** (page 128). Color and cut out the rabbit; then mount it on a background. Encourage children to fingerpaint pictures of garden foods. When the paint dries, instruct children to cut out their pictures. Mount each child's food on the board and label it with cutout letters.

Doris Hautala, Washington Elementary, Ely, MN

Honor your kindergarten grads with this display. Hang a real graduation robe on a hanger; then attach the hanger to the board. Arrange and pin the flowing robe to the board. Give each child a copy of the **graduate and cap patterns** (page 129). Have him color the graduate to resemble himself and then color and glue on the cap. Display each proud graduate on the board; then have him write his name near his cutout.

W. L. Harris, St. Petersburg, FL

No matter how you slice them, these watermelons make a luscious display. When each child has enjoyed a slice of real watermelon, have him wash and dry the seeds. Have him glue a pink half circle to a slightly larger green half circle; then glue the real seeds onto the paper slice. Write on his watermelon slice as each child dictates his summer plans. Before attaching it to a background, tear a bite out of the slice. Add paper vines and a title to complete the display.

Andrea Esposito—Preschool, VA/YMCA Child Care Center, Brooklyn, NY

# Red, White, Blue— And You!

This star-spangled display is perfect for a patriotic celebration! In advance, glue a blue rectangle in the upper left corner of a large white sheet of butcher paper. Then invite each child to make red handprints to resemble the stripes that are on the U.S. flag. Next, have each child paint a couple of white fingerprints to resemble stars. It's red, white, blue, and YOU!

Jan Grothe
St. Luke's Preschool
Federal Way, WA

Carol Frith—Gr. K
Tallulah Academy Kindergarten
Tallulah, LA

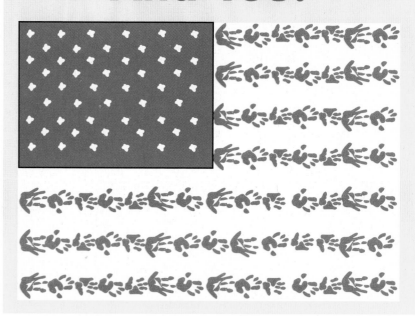

This board will inspire onlookers. Cut 4" x 18" strips of white paper—enough to make a border. Have children sponge-paint red and blue stars on the strips. Staple the strips around a blue background. Next, have children sponge-paint red, white, and blue heart shapes on the backs of light blue sentence strips. On another sheet of paper, have each child write and illustrate why he loves his country. Mount each page under the child's strip.

# Anytime

Happy birthday! Use a party-themed border to trim a bright background. Write the birthday song on a piece of chart paper, as shown, and then laminate it. Have each child color and cut out a copy of the **picture frame pattern** (page 130). Then attach each child's picture to his frame. Staple the song, student photos, and balloon cutouts to the board. Write each child's name on a separate sentence strip. On a child's special day, pin his name to the open space in the chart and let the celebration begin.

Beverly Nordin—Gr. K, Sykes Elementary. Jackson, MS

Happy birthday to you, and you, and you! Enlarge the **birthday cake pattern** (page 131). Color, cut out, and laminate the pattern. Write each child's name and birthdate on a different construction paper balloon. Then mount the cake and the balloons to make this festive birthday display.

Denise Brown—4- and 5-year-olds, America's Children Of Oakmoor, Des Moines, IA

60

# Special Days to Remember

This elephant is 100 percent faithful to remind you of these special days! Copy the **gift box, nameplate, and gift tag patterns** (page 133) to make a set for each child. Then color and cut out a copy of the **elephant pattern** (page 132) and mount it on a wall. Using helium or construction paper balloons, title the display as shown. Have each child decorate his gift, add his nameplate, and program the gift tag with the date of his birth. Post each gift near that child's birth month; then top it off with a real bow.

adapted from an idea by
Heather Tulak—Gr. K
Labadieville Primary
Labadieville, LA

This smiling gumball machine welcomes student birthdays in a special way. Enlarge, color, and cut out the **gumball machine pattern** (page 134); then post it on the board. Cut a small gumball from colorful construction paper for each child. Label the gumballs with student names and birthdays; then attach them inside the machine. Place a student's gumball in the slot on his birthday. Celebrate summer birthdays during the final days of the school year.

Help your students enjoy the sweet taste of success with this incentive display. Enlarge the **gumball machine pattern** (page 134). After coloring and cutting it out, mount the machine on a small bulletin board. Cut out a large circle from construction paper for each child. Label the gumballs with students' names and staple them on the board as shown. Each time a student improves in a skill or reaches a goal, he gets a sticker to place on his gumball. When five stickers have been earned, the student receives a special prize.

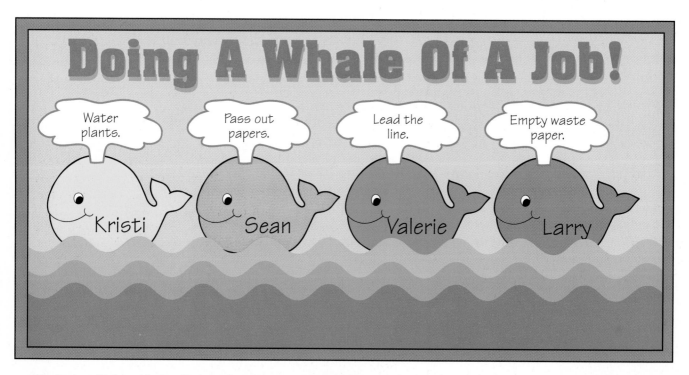

Students will do a whale of a job when you use this fun jobs bulletin board! Label colorful **whale patterns** (page 135) with students' names. Label **white spout patterns** (page 135) with classroom jobs. Attach several rows of blue corrugated border for water. Change the whales weekly.

Launch good behavior with this display. Duplicate and personalize a **hot-air balloon pattern** (page 136) for each child. Then enlarge the pattern and trace it on colorful paper. Cut out all the patterns. Mount the large balloon on a blue background with five rows of clouds. For each day that a child demonstrates good behavior, advance his personalized balloon to the next row of clouds. When a child gets to the top row of clouds, reward him!

Jennifer Woods—Gr. K
Alma Primary
Alma, AR

Need to motivate students to practice quiet-as-a-mouse behavior? Make this display! Duplicate the **mouse and cheese patterns** (page 137) to make a class supply; then personalize a mouse for each child. Display the mice and cheese slices along with the title shown. Each time a child demonstrates quiet behavior, invite him to add a small white sticker dot to his cheese. When he's earned ten stickers, reward him with a stick of string cheese. Yum!

Cathy Peterson—Gr. K
Old Suwanee Christian School
Buford, GA

Using fabric paint, paint a racetrack on a hemmed piece of fabric. Along the track, attach the hook sides of a quantity of Velcro fastener. Make a class supply of the **racecar pattern** (page 138) and a desired number of the **gas pump pattern** (page 138). Laminate and then cut out the patterns. Personalize the cars; then use the loop sides of Velcro fastener to randomly attach them to the track. Use additional pieces of Velcro fasteners to secure the gas pumps at distances around the track. A child moves her car around the track as appropriate behaviors are displayed. When her car stops at a pump, fill 'er up with a treat!

Libby Mackman
Lowell Elementary
Madison, WI

Good character shines with this display! Mount a large **lighthouse pattern** (page 139) on a bulletin board. Draw beams of light extending from the top. Label each one with a desirable character trait; then add a symbol to represent each trait. Add the title shown, as well as blue paper waves below. Make a **sailboat pattern** (page 139) for each child and place it "in" the water. As a child exhibits each trait, add a sticker showing the relevant symbol to her sail.

Shannon Adams—Gr. K, Waxahachie Faith Family Academy, Waxahachie, TX

Foster self-esteem and keep skills right on track with this board. Mount a large **engine pattern** (page 140) on a wall or board. Attach the caption to a smoke puff made of batting. For each skill that you'd like to track, add a labeled construction paper train car. As each child masters or makes progress with a given skill, write his name on the appropriate train car. Keep chuggin' along!

Michele D. Romeiser—Gr. K, Childtime Child Center, Fairport, NY

Here's a convenient showcase for your little artists' masterpieces. Using bulletin board border, divide a board or wall into sections according to the number of children in your class. (Add extra sections for new students, if desired.) Write each child's name on a sentence strip; then laminate the strips. Mount the names as shown. When each child completes a work of art, she'll know just where to display it.

Diane Joseph—Gr. K, Bayou Vista Elementary, Morgan City, LA

Recognize the hard work of your young buckaroos with this rootin'-tootin' display! Enlarge and color the **cowboy pattern** (page 141); then cut it out and mount it on the board. For fun, pin a real bandana kerchief on the cowboy. Duplicate the **hat pattern** (page 142) on construction paper for each child. A student cuts out her hat; then she labels it with her name and one or two sentences about a rootin'-tootin' terrific thing she's done.

With this board, children and their parents will be buzzing about their kindergarten accomplishments. For each child, duplicate the **bee pattern** (page 143) on construction paper. Have each child color his bee; then write his name on the flag. Then have each child write about and illustrate some of the things he has learned in kindergarten. Display each child's page on the board along with his bee page topper.

Adapted from an idea by Denise Westgard—Gr. K
Shiloh Christian School, Bismarck, ND

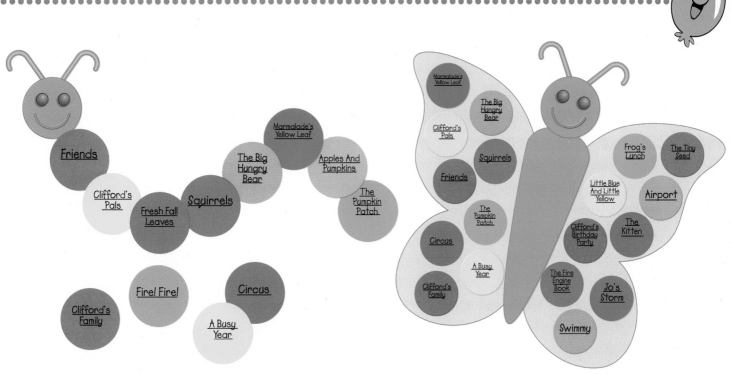

To create this display, cut a supply of large construction paper circles. Add pom-pom eyes, a yarn mouth, and pipe cleaner antennae to one circle to resemble a caterpillar's head. Attach the circle to a wall. Each time a book is read aloud, write the title on a new circle; then attach it to the wall to create an ever-growing caterpillar. In the spring, remove the circles from the wall and rearrange them on a large butterfly shape. A year of reading takes flight!

Kathryn D. Small—Three- and Four-Year-Olds, Parkminster Preschool, Rochester, NY

Cackle, cackle, cluck, cluck! This cheerful chick creates quite a spectacle as her mound of eggs grows higher and higher. Enlarge the **hen and nest patterns** (page 144). After coloring and cutting out the patterns, mount them on the board. Duplicate a supply of construction paper **egg patterns** (page 144). Explain to students that they will earn an egg for each book that they read. Challenge the class to raise the hen to the ceiling. When the hen reaches this monumental height, surprise students with an "egg-ceptional" treat!

## Piggin' Out on Books

This mouthwatering display keeps track of young readers' progress! Duplicate the **bowl, topping, and ice-cream patterns** (page 146) to make a class supply. Mount the bowls, each labeled with a different child's name, on a bulletin board or wall around a large **pig pattern** (page 145). Then add the title shown. Enlist the help of students in coloring the ice-cream scoops and toppings. As each child reads a book or completes a book report, add an ingredient to her bowl. At a predetermined time, reward your readers with an ice-cream party and let them eat the ingredients they've earned!

Stacy Wingen—Gr. K
Howard Elementary
Howard, SD

# Have a Ball—
# READ!

Hey, batter, batter—hit *these* balls! Mount a bat and a cap cutout on a board; then add a title. (If desired, pin on a real cap and use a Velcro fastener to attach a toy baseball bat.) Then photocopy a supply of construction paper **baseball patterns** (page 147). When a child reads a book, write that title on a half sheet of paper. Then give him a baseball cutout and have him write his name on it. Help him display his book and ball on the board. Reading scores big, right off the bat!

adapted from an idea by Jane M. Kjosen, Edgewood Elementary School, Greenfield, WI

Round up enthusiasm for reading by featuring youngsters' favorite books in this eye-catching display. Enlarge and color a **cactus pattern** (page 148); then mount it on a background along with a caption. Attach a book cover inside a ropelike lasso created from twisted strips of bulletin-board paper. Read 'em, cowpoke!

Amy Barsanti—Four-Year-Olds
St. Andrew's Preschool
Nags Head, NC

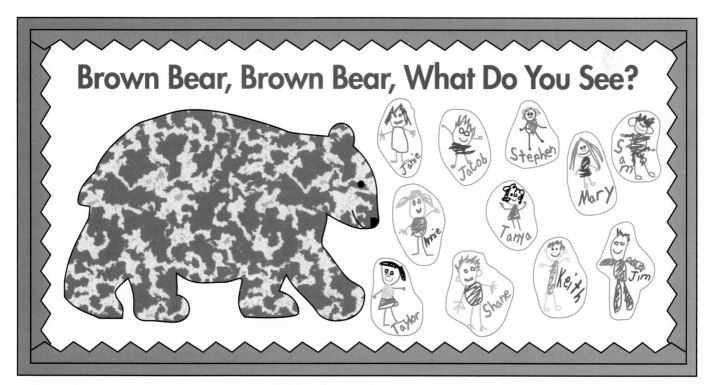

Follow up a reading of *Brown Bear, Brown Bear, What Do You See?* by making this board. Use an opaque projector to trace a large **bear pattern** (page 149) on a sheet of butcher paper. Invite children to sponge-paint the bear; then cut it out. Mount the bear and the title on the board. Have each child draw a self-portrait, write his name on it, and cut it out. Then use the finished display to guide choral chanting inspired by the book's text.

Adapted from an idea by Judy Kelley, Wayland, MA

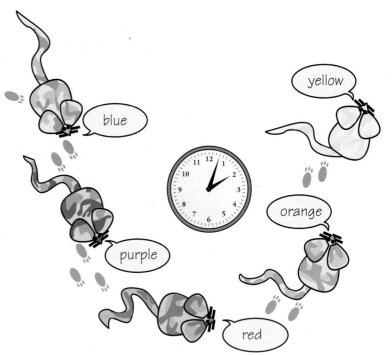

Follow up a reading of *Mouse Paint* by Ellen Stoll Walsh with this wall display. Have each child fingerpaint a large sheet of paper with a color of her choice. If desired, provide only primary colors and have the child mix two colors to get her color choice. After the paint dries, provide **mouse body and ear pattern** (page 150) templates for the children to trace and cut out. Direct each youngster to cut out a squiggly tail from the leftover paper. Help each child glue the pieces together to create a mouse, adding paper whiskers and thumbprint eyes. Attach the painted mice to a wall along a trail of mouse tracks. Eeeek!

Carol Fitzgibbons
Penn Yan Elementary
Penn Yan, NY

Follow up a reading of *Stellaluna* by Janell Cannon or culminate a unit of study on bats with this display. Have each child stuff a black paper bag and staple it closed. Then direct her to cut out construction paper eyes and fangs and glue them on the bag. Next, have the child cut out a copy of black **wing patterns** (page 151) and tape them to the sides of her bag. Mount the bats on a night sky background along with students' dictation about bats or about their favorite parts of the story.

Felice Kestenbaum—Gr. K, Goosehill Primary, Cold Spring Harbor, NY

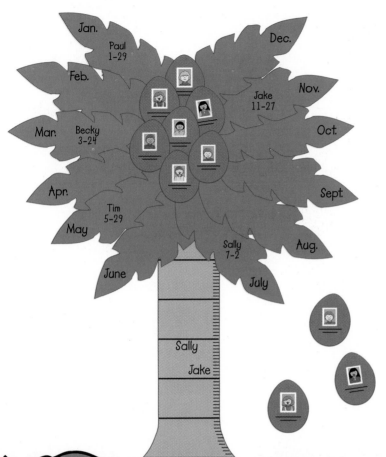

Cut a five-foot-tall tree trunk and 12 palm fronds from bulletin board paper. Label each frond with a different month. Mark inch indications on the trunk, drawing a line across the trunk every 12 inches. Laminate the pieces; then attach them to a wall, being sure to place the trunk even with the base of the wall. For each child personalize and attach a school photo to a coconut cutout; then attach the cutouts to the center of the fronds. Using a wipe-off marker, write each child's birthday on the appropriate frond and indicate his height on the trunk.

Terri Johnson—Three- and Four-Year-Olds
Learning Tree of America, Carrollton, GA

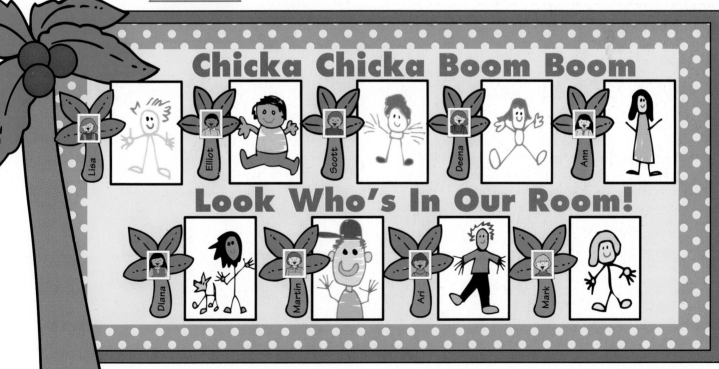

Here's an enticing display. Take a photo of each child and have him draw a self-portrait. Mount a border of pink paper and yellow dots. Attach each child's photo to the center of a different, personalized colored construction paper **coconut tree pattern** (page 152). Mount the tree near his self-portrait. Add a very large, construction paper coconut tree and a title near the board. And be sure to share the book with your group

Felice Kestenbaum—Gr. K, Goosehill Primary, Cold Spring Harbor, NY

# The Princess and the Pea

Enhance your fairy-tale unit with this creative display that integrates literature, art, and math! After sharing your favorite version of *The Princess and the Pea,* give each child a long strip of bulletin board paper. Instruct the child to paint a pattern of his choice on this paper mattress. Make a bed by using three strips of dark-colored bulletin board paper. Stack and tape each student's mattress above the bed's base. Then invite one student volunteer to paint a princess to rest on the top mattress and another volunteer to make a pea for the bottom mattress. Just perfect!

Valerie Jewell—Gr. K
Chattahoochee Elementary
Duluth, GA

Follow up a reading of *Miss Mary Mack,* adapted by Mary Ann Hoberman, by making this display. First, print the verses of the rhyme on sheets of writing paper. Have one small group of students illustrate each verse. Display the verses and illustrations around a three-dimensional Miss Mary Mack. To make her body, stuff a large black plastic bag with paper, adding additional sections of another bag for arms. Tape yellow yarn inside an old hat for the head. Add stuffed black panty-hose, real shoes, gloves, and a jump rope as shown. Crumpled pieces of aluminum foil will serve nicely as silver buttons, all down her back, back, back!

Linda Newman—Gr. K
Washington Hebrew Early Childhood Center
Potomac, MD

Create a forest of word recognition with these word family trees. Cut large tree shapes from bulletin board paper. Glue die-cut letters to the trunk of each tree to designate its word family. Laminate the trees and attach them to a classroom wall. Have youngsters write different words on seasonal shapes and then tape them to the correct tree. (If desired, use two marker colors as shown.) We're growing reading skills!

Sandra Miller—Gr. K
Mt. Calvary School
Erie, PA

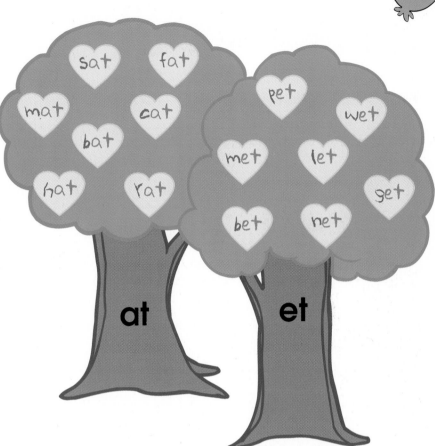

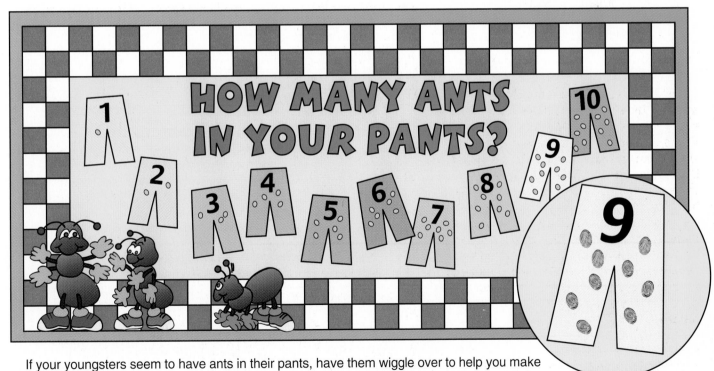

If your youngsters seem to have ants in their pants, have them wiggle over to help you make this summertime display. Cut a class supply of paper **pants patterns** (page 153); then label each shape with a numeral from one to ten. (Write each numeral at least once.) Ask each child to choose a pair of pants and to look at the numeral. Then have him press the corresponding number of fingerprint ants onto the pants. Sequence the pants before mounting them on a titled board along with ant characters.

Pamela Chandler, Clifton Park, NY

# The Learning Window

Open up a window of learning possibilities with this unique display idea. Attach letter, number, or shape cutouts to a window labeled "The Learning Window." For a spark of excitement, keep the curtains closed until, during a circle time, you reveal newly added cutouts.

Carol Denny—Three- and Four-Year-Olds
First Baptist Church
Conyers, GA

Nothing's fishy about the creativity involved in making these shapely fish! Provide youngsters with glue and construction paper geometric shapes in a variety of colors and sizes. Have students use the shapes to create colorful fish. Display the fish on a background along with paper seaweed and coral. Yes, that is a new species of triangle fish that you see!

Kathy McCauley—PreK, St. Patrick Interparish School, Gainesville, FL

Here's patterning practice that results in quite a remarkable quilt design! Have each child make a tempera-paint handprint on a six-inch square of paper. Then ask him to glue two colors of two-inch paper squares in an AB pattern on another six-inch square. Glue all the student-made squares onto bulletin board paper to complete the project. If this cozy quilt is a big hit with your children, have them create another one in a few weeks, varying the colors and the quilt pattern.

Tarie Curtiss—Gr. K
Arthur Road Elementary School
Solon, OH

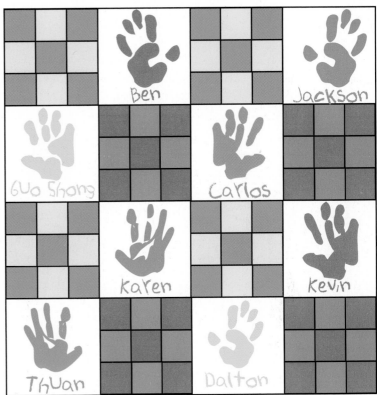

The fishing is just right in this spot! Create this scene on a bulletin board. Lightly stuff plastic grocery bags behind a loosely mounted paper sun and cloud. Label each pond with a different heading according to your group's abilities. Duplicate the **fish patterns** (page 154) several times on construction paper. Laminate, program, and cut out each fish. Store the fish in a net or bag. Have children sort the fish and use Sticky-Tac to mount them in the appropriate ponds.

With this display, your students—and all your visitors—will know what's up in your classroom! Using an opaque projector, enlarge the **bear pattern** (page 155) on colored construction paper. Color in details; then cut out and laminate the pattern. Also cut out and laminate several construction paper balls. Program each ball with a skill or topic that you're currently studying. Mount all the pieces on a classroom wall or board; then use a permanent marker to write a title on the bear's buttons.

Diane Pittman
Tina-Avalon School
Tina, MO

Color your world with these giant paintbrushes. Each time you study a color, cut a large **paintbrush pattern** (page 156) from that color of bulletin board paper and label it with the corresponding color word. Invite children to cut out magazine pictures of items that are that color; then have them glue the pictures onto the paintbrush. Display these giant paintbrushes on a wall along a hallway.

As a variation, cut paintbrushes out of construction paper. Then, after youngsters have glued on pictures, bind the brushes together on a ring to make a class book.

adapted from an idea by Sandra Faulkner and Traci Baker—
  Four-Year-Olds
Kernersville Moravian Preschool
Kernersville, NC

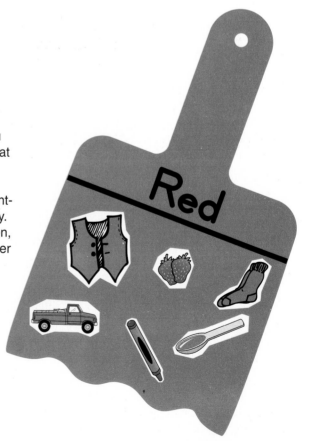

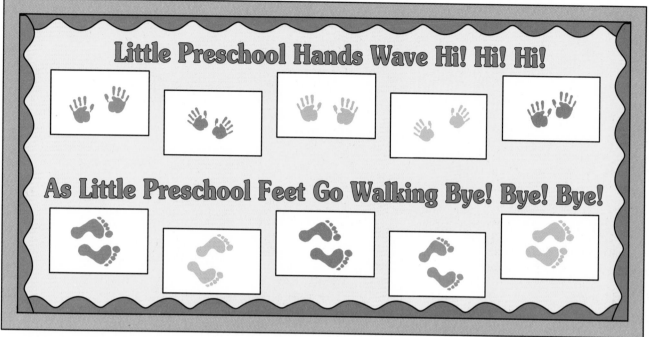

During your self-awareness study, set up this warm and welcoming display in a hallway. Mount students' handprints and footprints on a bulletin board as shown; then add the rhyme shown. As your preschoolers and other visitors pass the display, they won't be able to resist waving and smiling!

Jodi M. Kilburg, Bellevue Elementary School, Bellevue, IA

To create this display, post a construction paper **earth pattern** (page 105) and the title. Have each child craft a person from skin-toned construction paper. Mount all the craft people around the earth. From a basket of class names, have each child choose a classmate's name. Ask each child to write one good trait about the person he chose. Then have him cut out and glue his writing to a heart cutout. Mount the hearts around the earth.

adapted from an idea by Traci Schaffert, Hillcrest School, Morristown, NJ

# Where We Were Born

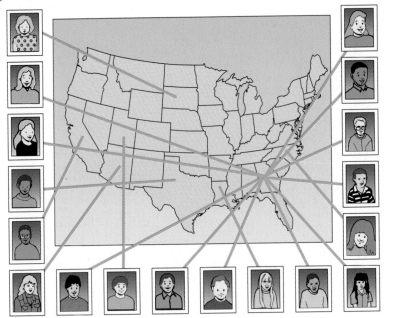

Make geography more personal as you help youngsters find their places of birth. Use an opaque projector to enlarge the **United States map pattern** (page 157). (Use a world map too, if needed). Attach the map to your classroom wall. Then post individual photos of your students around the map. Send a letter home to parents requesting their child's place of birth. Then, as the information comes in, use yarn to link each child to his birthplace. This display is sure to spark lots of conversation.

Leslie O'Donnell—Gr. K
Sedalia Park School
Marietta, GA

Sarah is marvelous because she likes to read.

Boost self-esteem with this picture-perfect display. For each student, decoratively cut around a brightly colored sheet of construction paper. To each sheet, attach a photo of a child and write "[Student's name] is marvelous because…." Have each child complete his sentence starter; then mount the completed projects on a board. Marvelous!

Joree King—Gr. K, Killarney Elementary, Orlando, FL

Here's a display that will go perfectly with your unit about families. Ask each child's family to attach photos of family members to a personalized sheet of construction paper. Mount the collected sheets together on a wall to resemble a quilt; then add a border. Invite parents to take a good look at your display of classy families.

Penny Horne—Preschool
University of Maine at Presque Isle Daycare Presque Isle, ME

Encourage your active bunch to follow playground safety rules. Enlarge the **monkey pattern** (page 158); then color, cut out, and mount the monkey on the board with paper branches and leaves as shown. After discussing playground safety rules, have each child illustrate one of the rules. Mount the drawings on green or purple paper. Duplicate the **paper topper pattern** (page 158) for each child on white paper. Have students color and cut out the toppers; then have them cut along the dotted line and slip the toppers on the corners of their drawings.

This display will have you singing, "We've got the sun in the morning and the moon at night!" Embellish a sun cutout with paper facial features and glitter; then add bottle-cap craters to a crescent-moon shape. Add cotton balls to cloud cutouts and foil streamers to metallic paper star cutouts. Mount all of the items on a board along with a tissue paper rainbow. Surround the items with students' dictated statements about day and night.

Nancy Barad—Four-Year-Olds, Bet Yeladim Preschool and Kindergarten, Columbia, MD

This amazing display grows right before your eyes! In advance, soak a supply of lima beans overnight. Provide each child with a resealable plastic bag half-filled with potting soil. Have the child plant two or three beans in the soil. Water the beans and then staple the bags to a bulletin board. Water the beans regularly and soon this display will sprout! If the beans begin to grow past the top of the board, mount plastic netting above the board to support the growing plants.

Jeri Gardner and Jane Schornhorst—Four-Year-Olds, Reid Memorial Preschool, Augusta, GA
Ann Becker—Four- and Five-Year-Olds, Deerwood Center, Milwaukee, WI

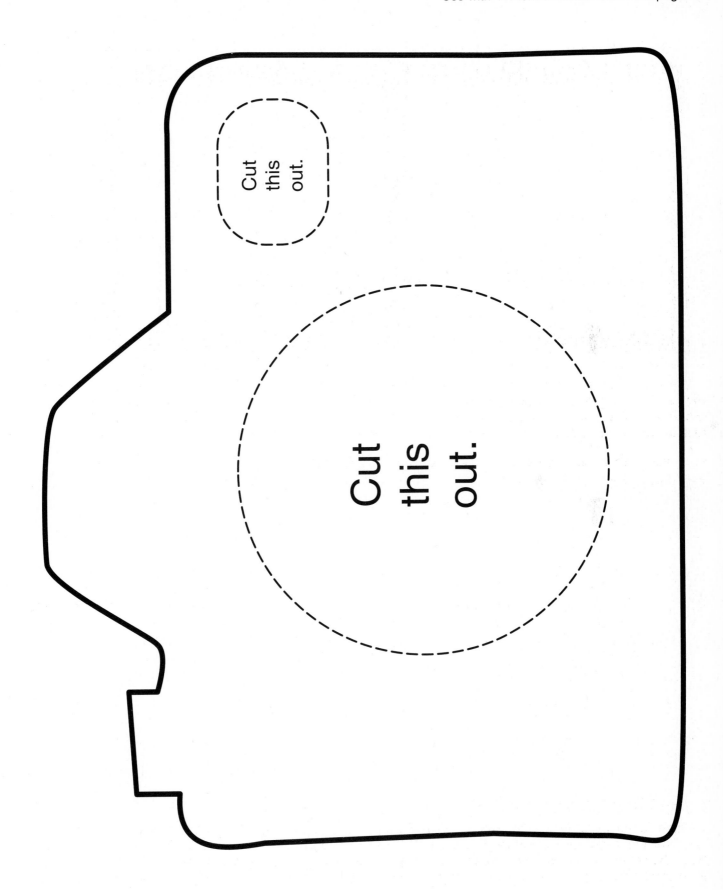

Cut
this
out.

Cut
this
out.

**Pattern**
Use with "I've Got a Hunch This Is a Bright
Bunch!" on page 4.

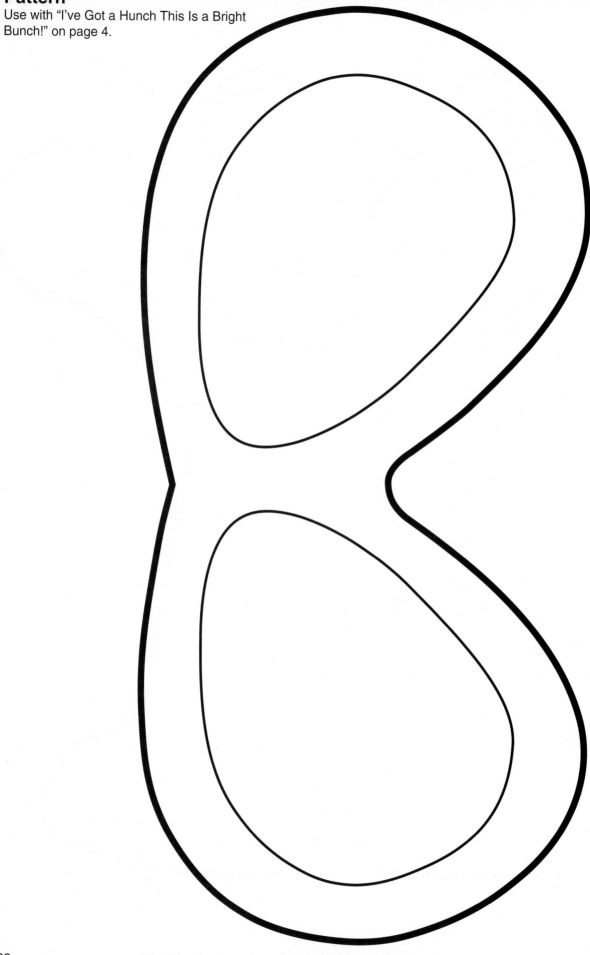

# Patterns
Use with "Welcome Color Friends!" on page 5.

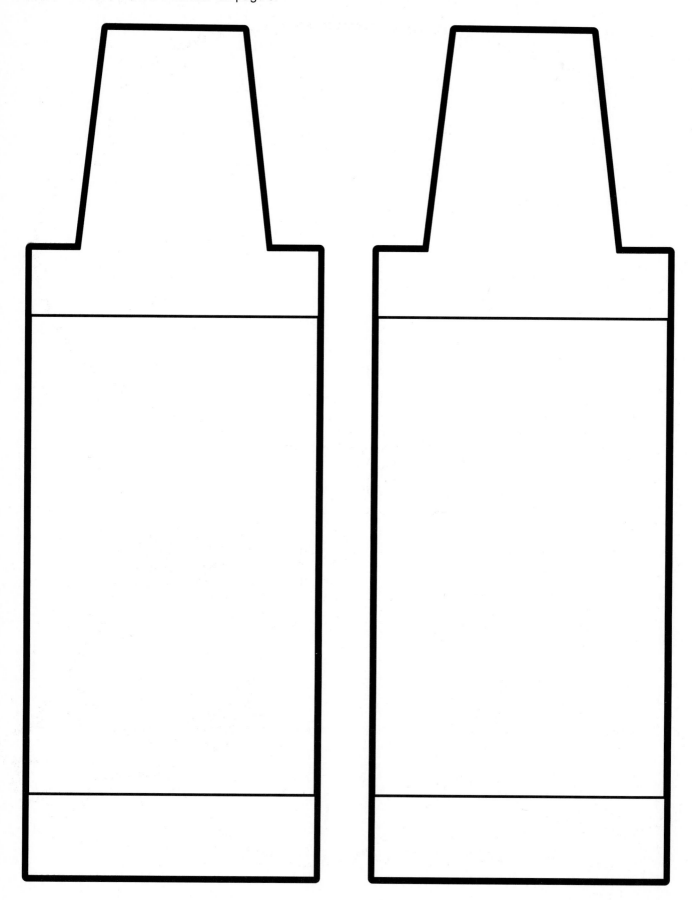

# Patterns
Use with "Preschoolers Are Popping Up Everywhere" on page 7.

# Pattern

Use with "My New Class Suits Me To a 'T'" on page 8.

**Pattern**
Use with "Guess 'Who-o-o'?" on page 10.

# Patterns
Use with "Falling Into Place" on page 12.

# Pattern

Use with the display on page 13.

# Patterns

Use with "'Corn-y' Counting" on page 16.

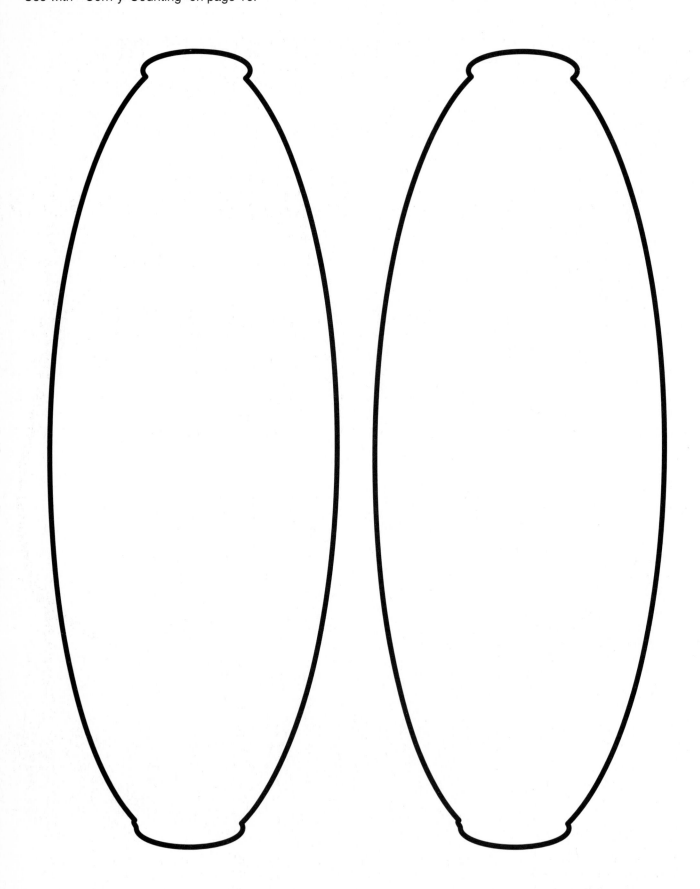

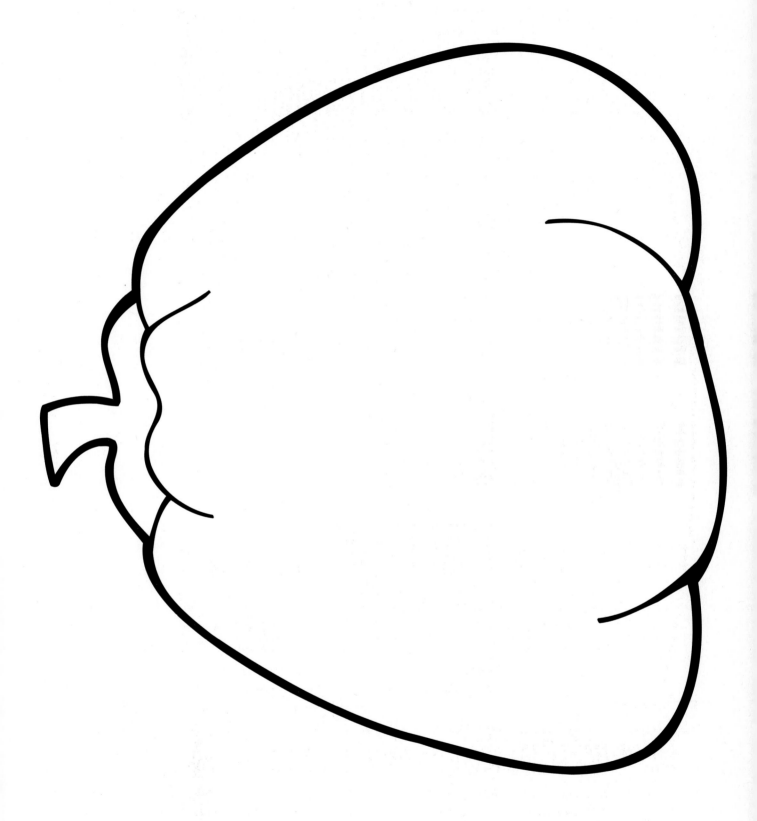

# Pattern

Use with the display on page 19.

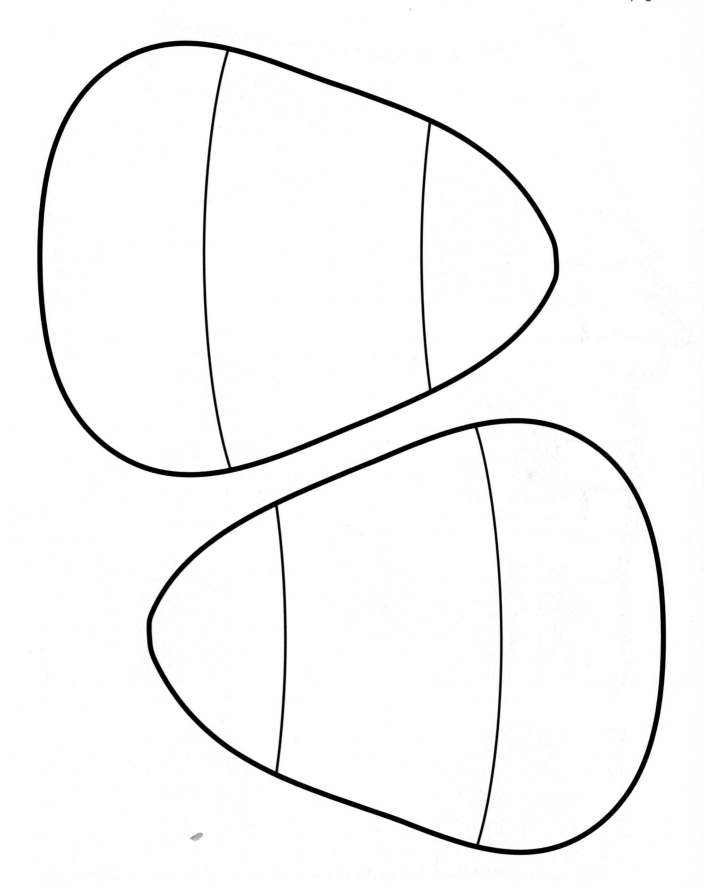

# Pattern
Use with "Turkey Dressing" on page 22.

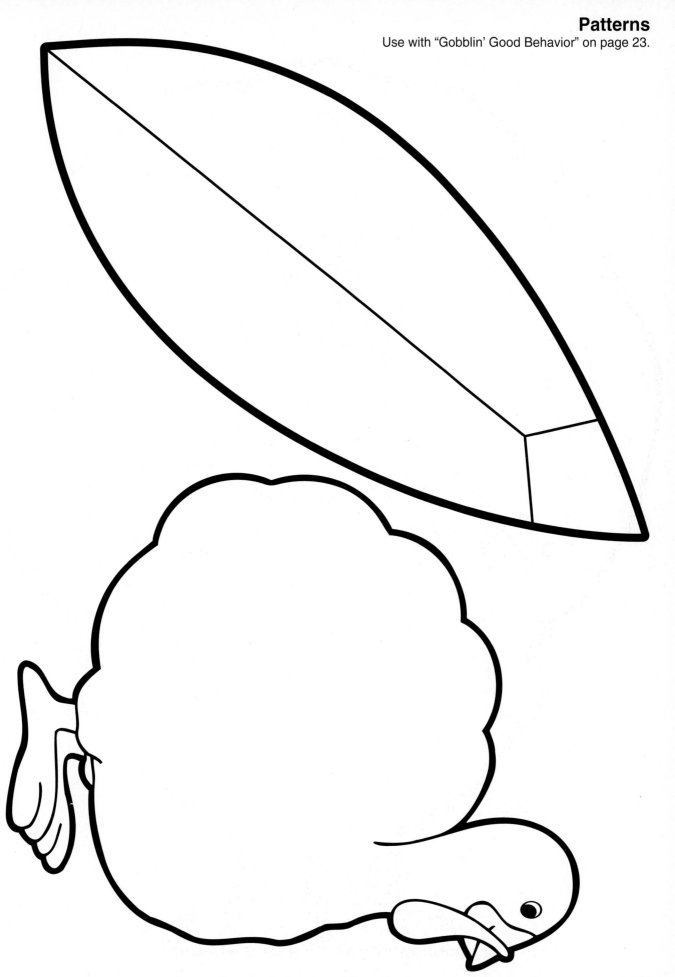

# Pattern

Use with "Whooo's Thankful?" on page 23.

# Pattern
Use with "Mittens Warm Hands. Friends Warm Hearts." on page 26.

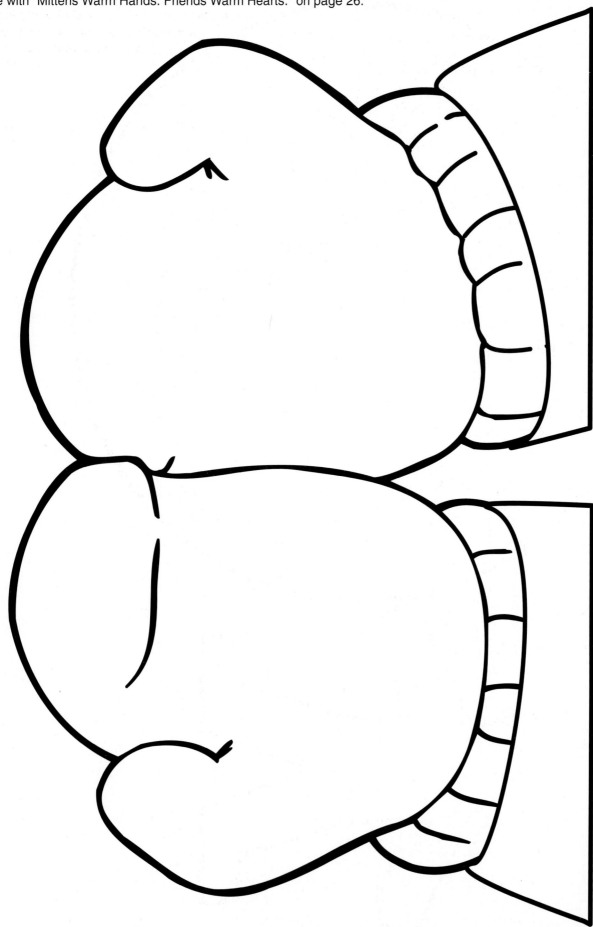

**Patterns**
Use with "Peace On Earth Begins With Me!"
on page 30, and "The Whole World's In Our
Hands" on page 56, and "Friendship
Makes the World Go Round"
on page 77.

**Pattern**
Use with "A Delightful Holiday
Glow" on page 31.

# Patterns

Use with "Miss Martin's Holiday Stars" on page 34.

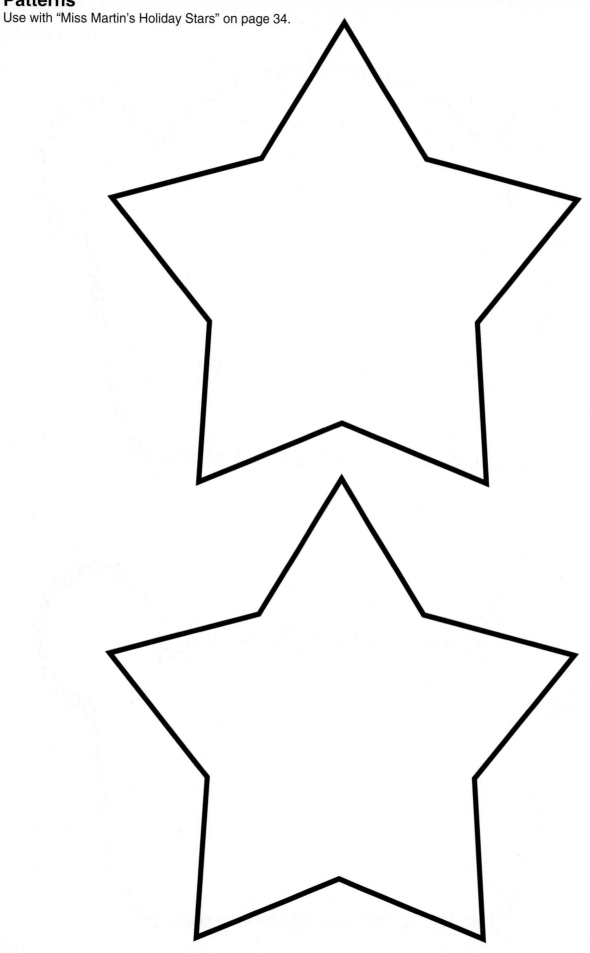

**Pattern**

Use with "The Children Were Nestled All Snug in Their Beds" on page 35.

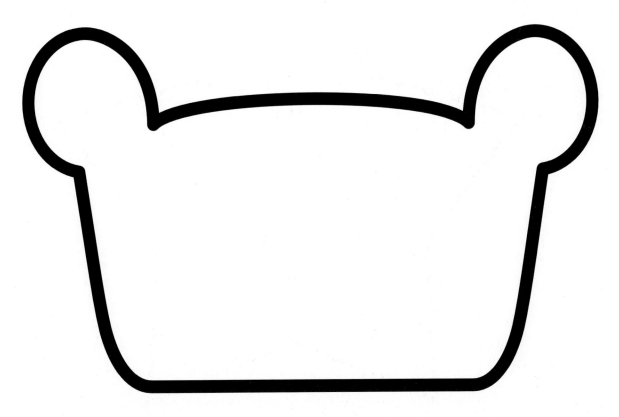

# Patterns

Use with "Our Little Angels" on page 37.

# Patterns
Use with "Happy New Year!" on page 39.

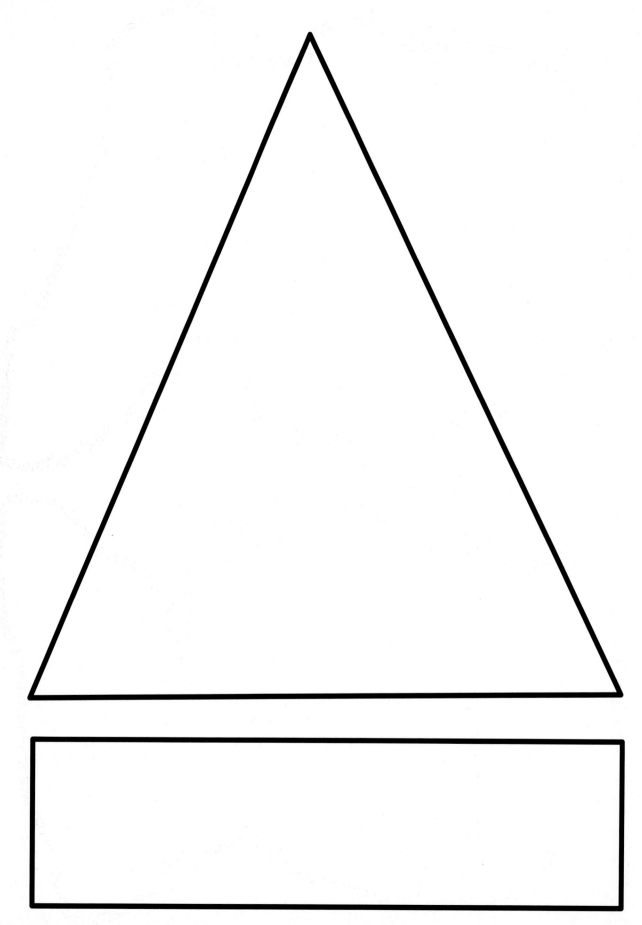

**George Washington**

**Abraham Lincoln**

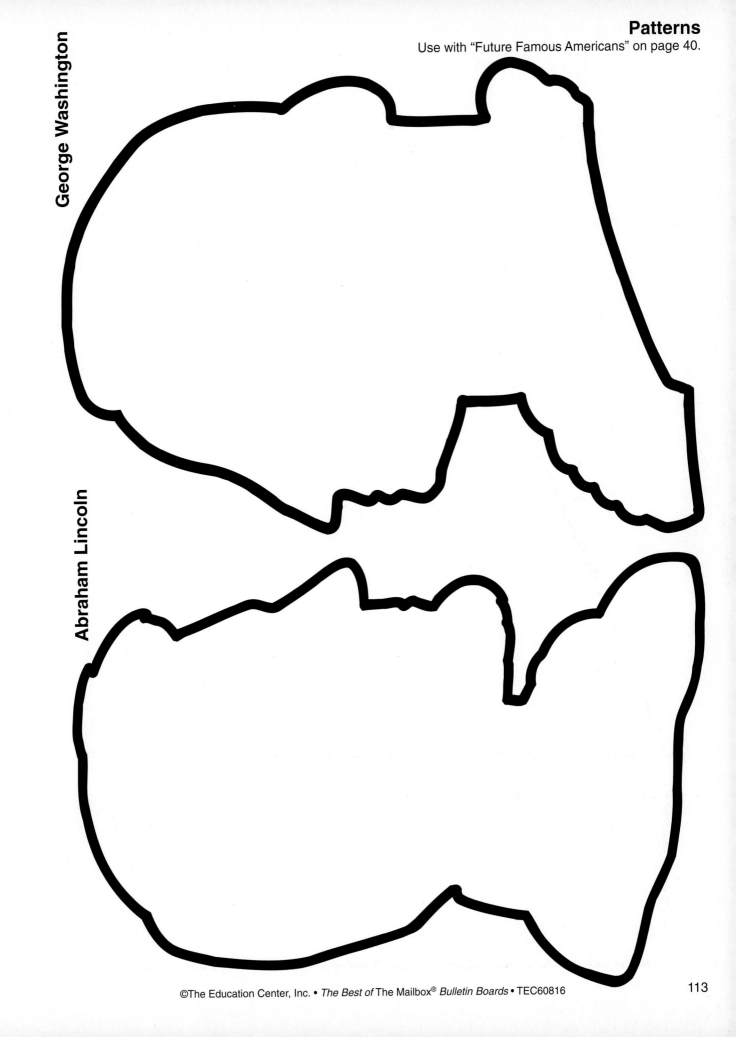

# Pattern
Use with "Love Letters" on page 41.

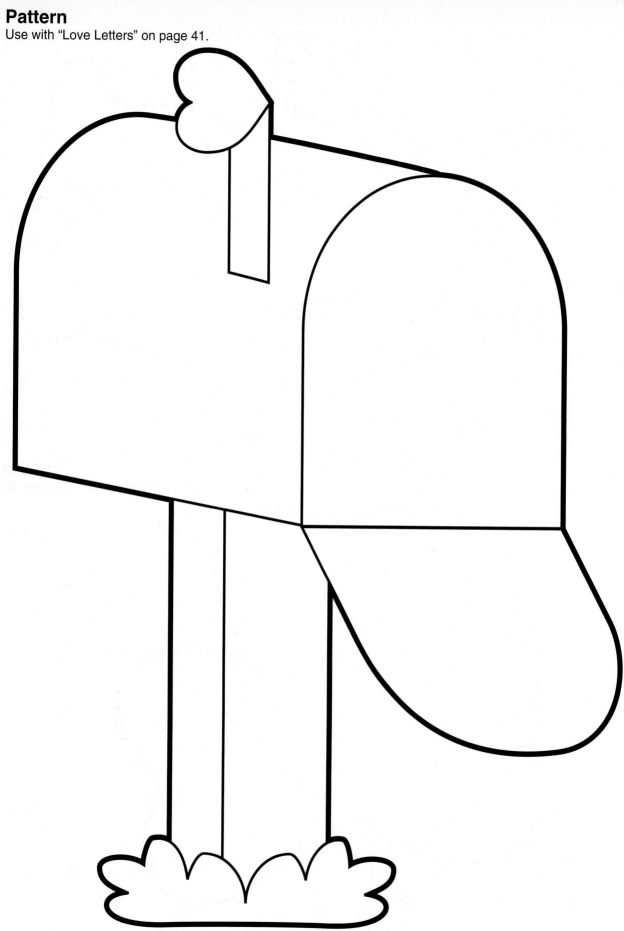

**Pattern**
Use with "Mrs. Guffey's Sweet Ones" on page 42.

**Pattern**
Use with "Green, Glorious Green!" on page 44.

# Patterns
Use with "We're More Precious Than Gold!" on page 44.

# Patterns

Use with "Sneaking Into Spring" on page 45.

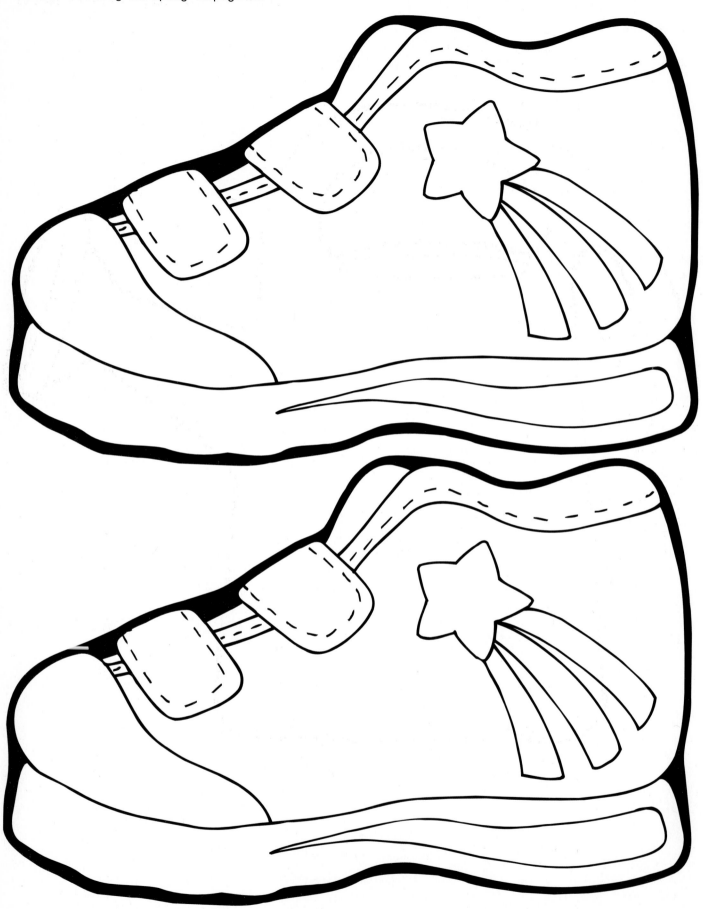

# Pattern
Use with "'Bee' A Reader!" on page 49.

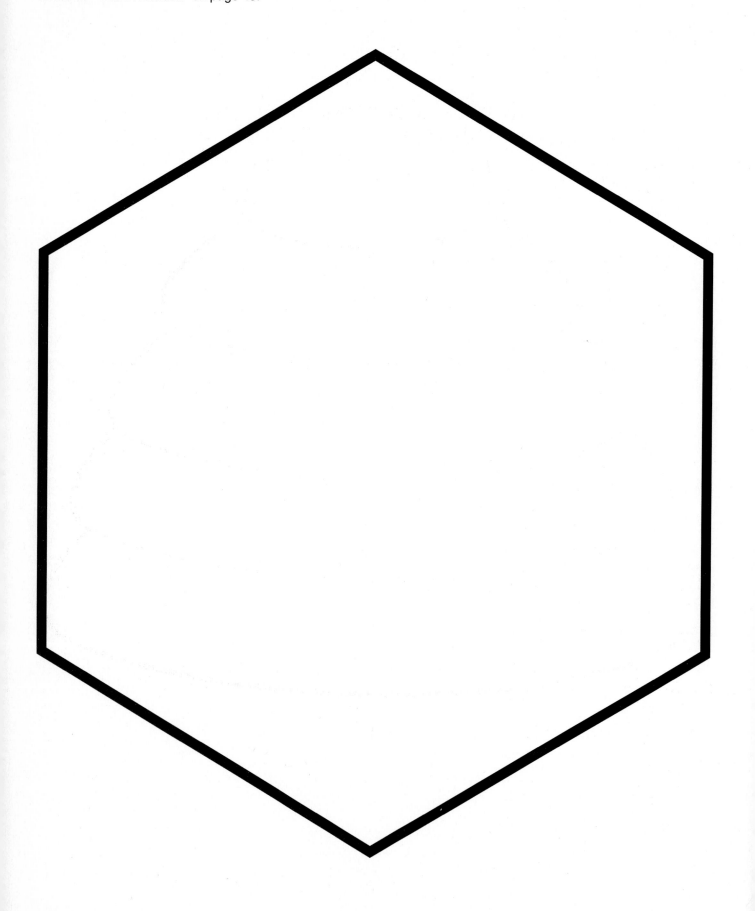

# Patterns

Use with "Windy Day Fun!" on page 50.

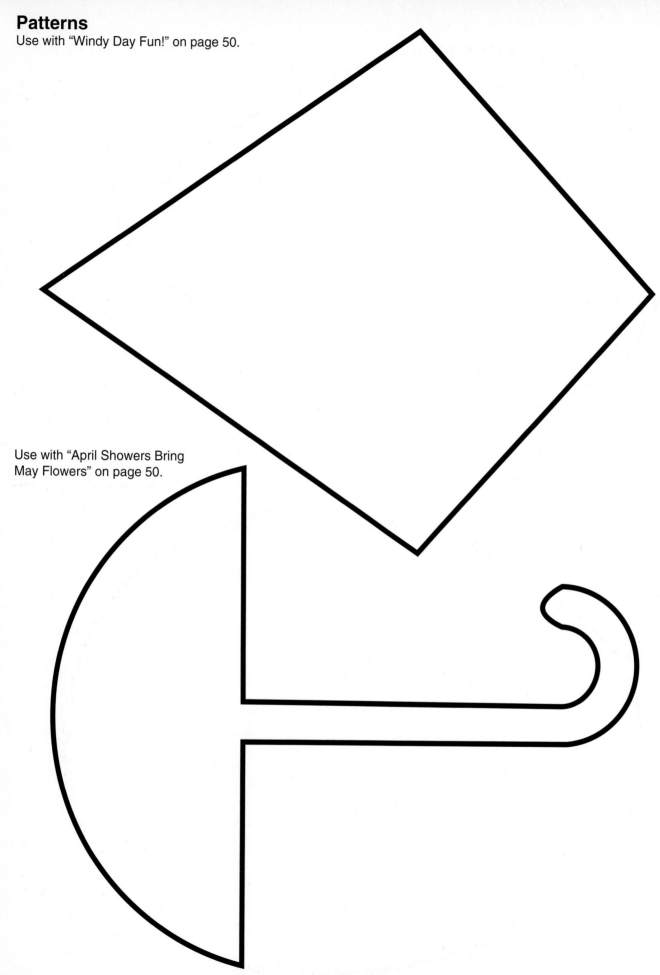

Use with "April Showers Bring May Flowers" on page 50.

Use with "'Chick' It Out!" and "Hunting for Patterns" on page 52.

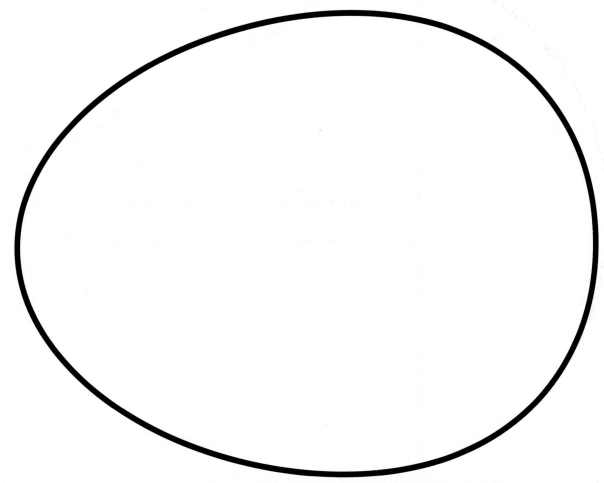

# Pattern

Use with the display on page 53.

# Pattern

Use with "'Egg-stra' Nice Eggs!" on page 54.

# Pattern

Use with "Mr. McGregor's Garden" on page 56.

# Patterns

Use with "Happy Birthday" on page 60.

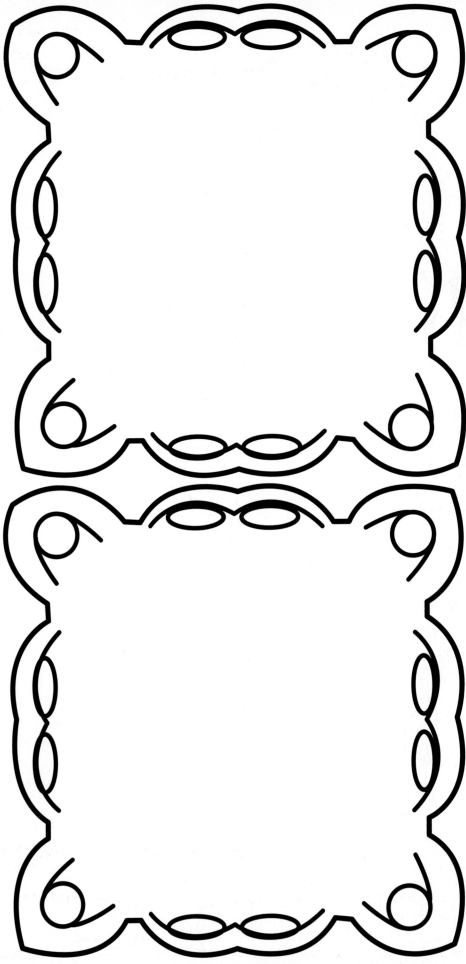

Use with "Happy Birthday to You!" on page 60.

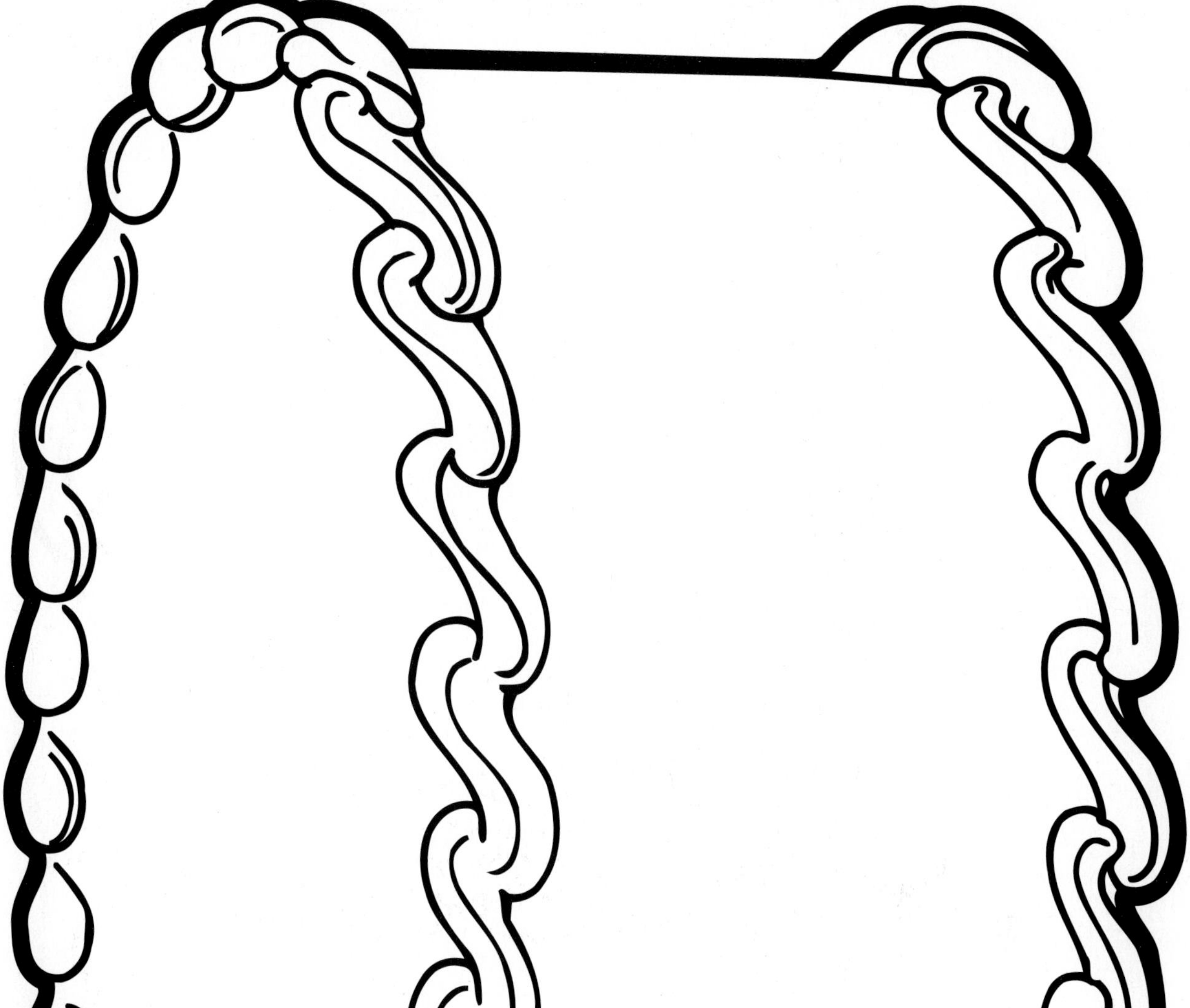

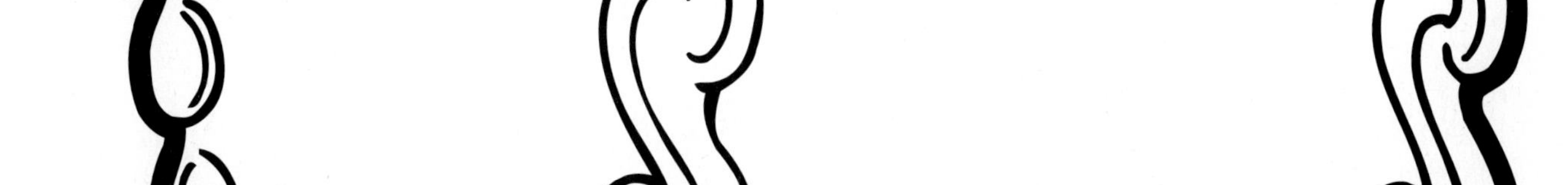

**Pattern**
Use with "Special Days to Remember" on page 61.

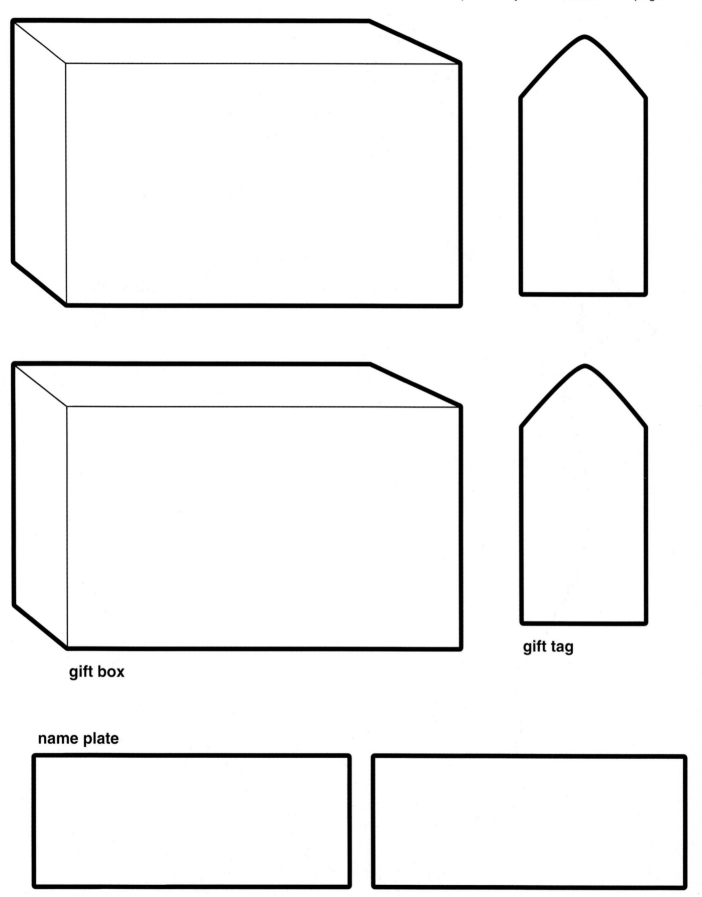

**gift box**

**gift tag**

**name plate**

**Pattern**
Use with "Goody, Goody Gumball! It's Your Birthday!" on page 61 and "We're on the Ball!" on page 62.

©The Education Center, Inc. • *The Best of* The Mailbox® *Bulletin Boards* • TEC60816

# Pattern

Use with "Up, Up and Away With Good
Behavior" on page 63.

# Patterns

Use with "Good Day Grand Prix" on page 64.

GALLONS

GAS

# Pattern

Use with "The I Can Express" on page 65.

# Pattern

Use with "We've Done Some Rootin'-Tootin' Terrific Things!" on page 66.

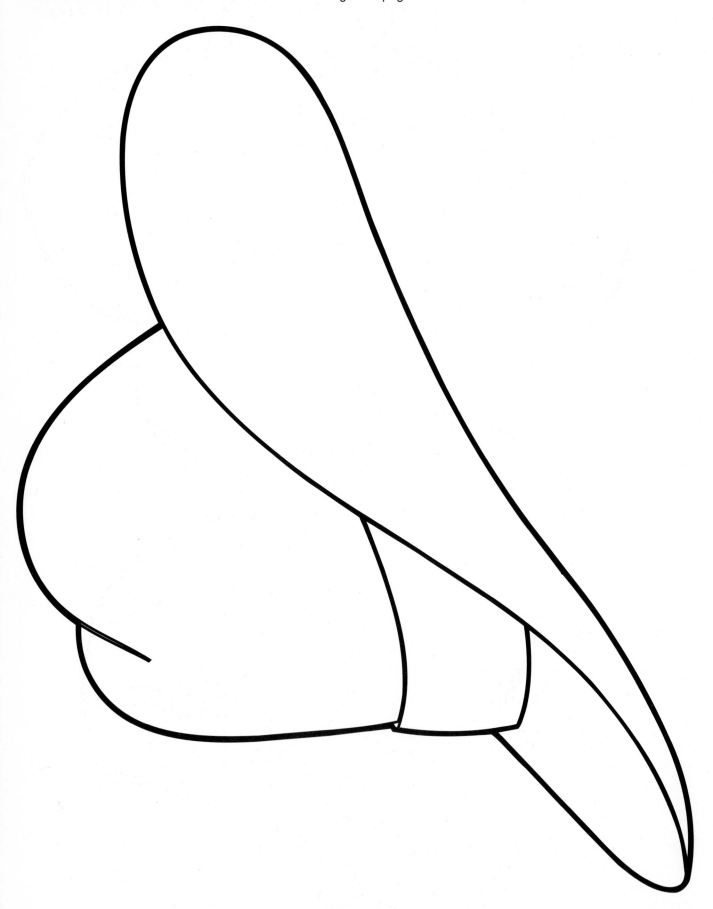

**Patterns**
Use with "We've Been Busy
Bees!" on page 66.

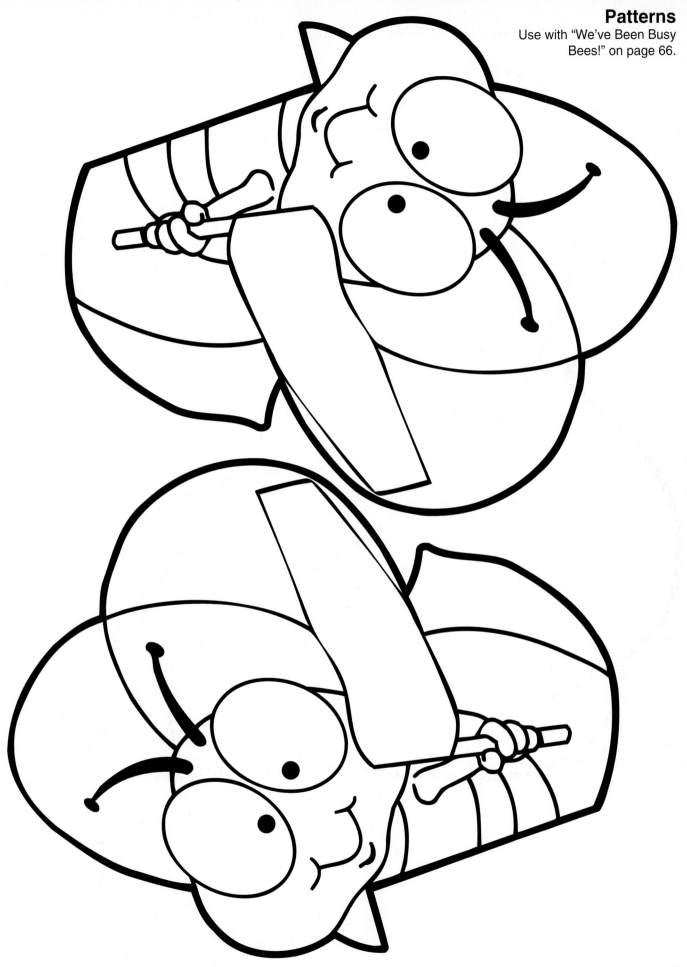

# Patterns

Enlarge and use with "Grade A Readers" on page 67.

Grade A Readers

# Patterns

Use with "Piggin' Out on Books" on page 68.

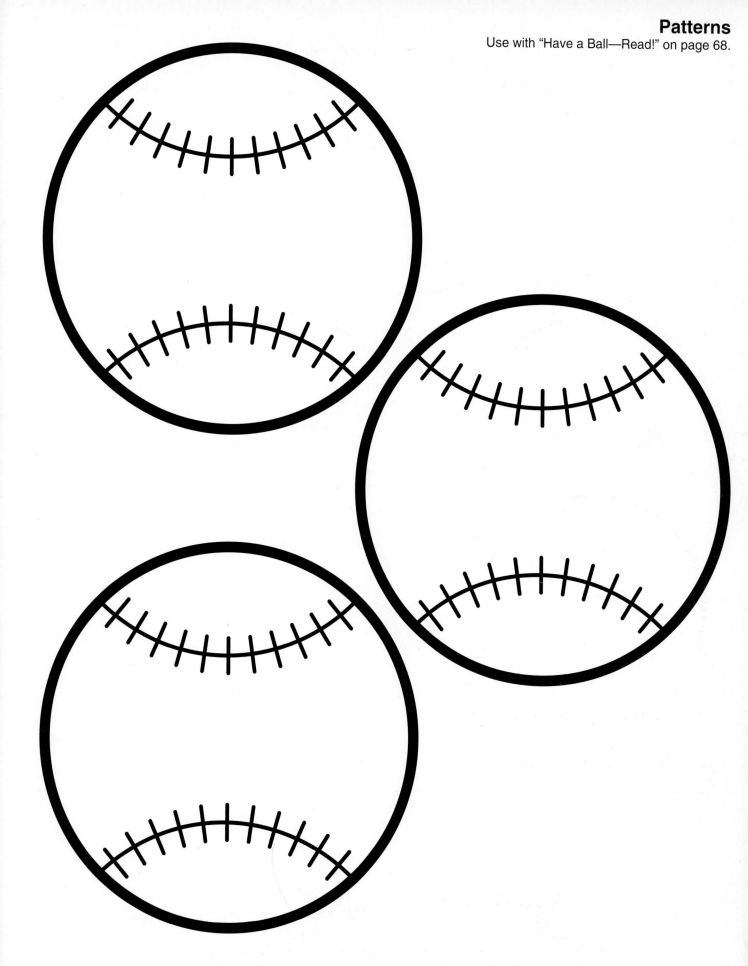

# Pattern
Use with "Howdy 'Book-a-roo'!" on page 69.

# Patterns
Use with the display on page 70.

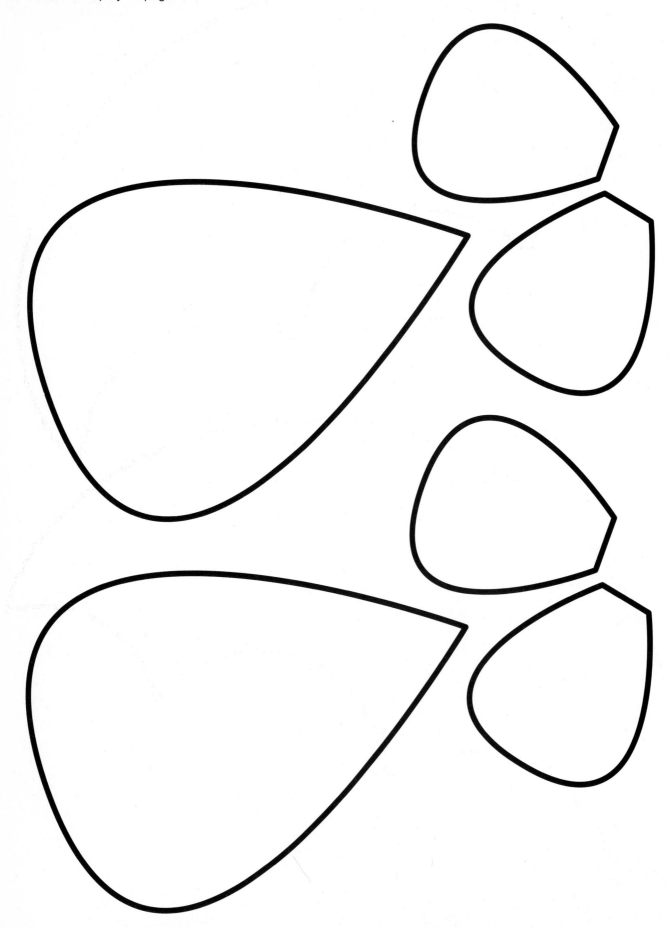

**Pattern**
Use with "Chicka Chicka Boom Boom" on page 71.

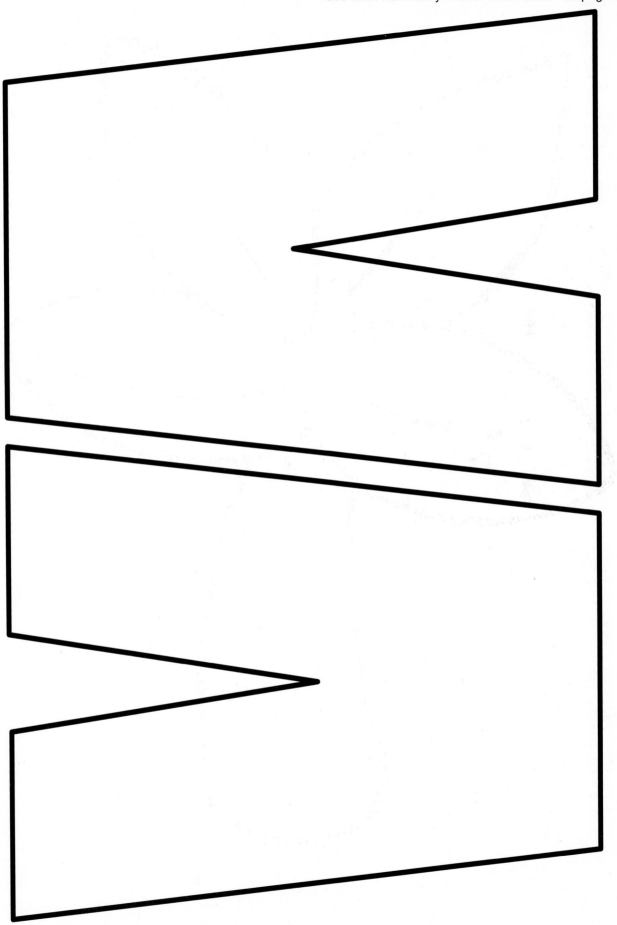

# Patterns
Use with "Schools of Fish" on page 75.

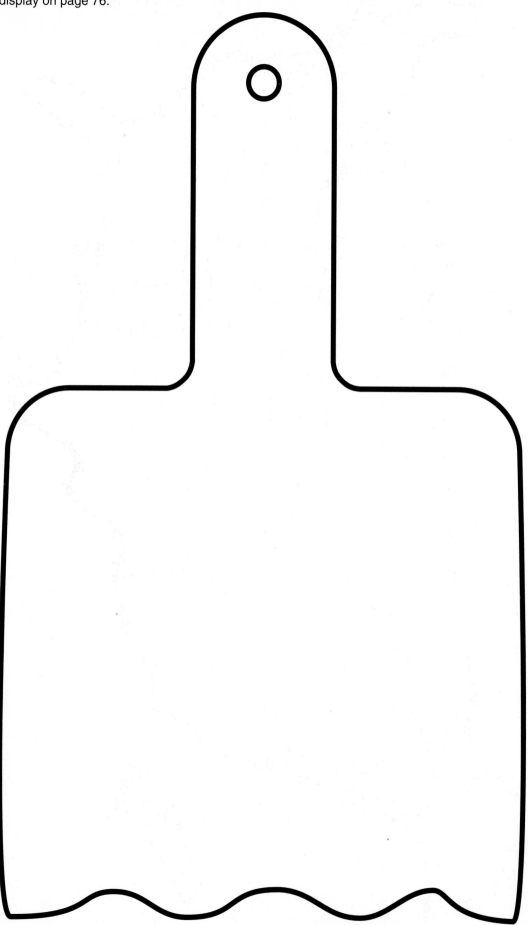

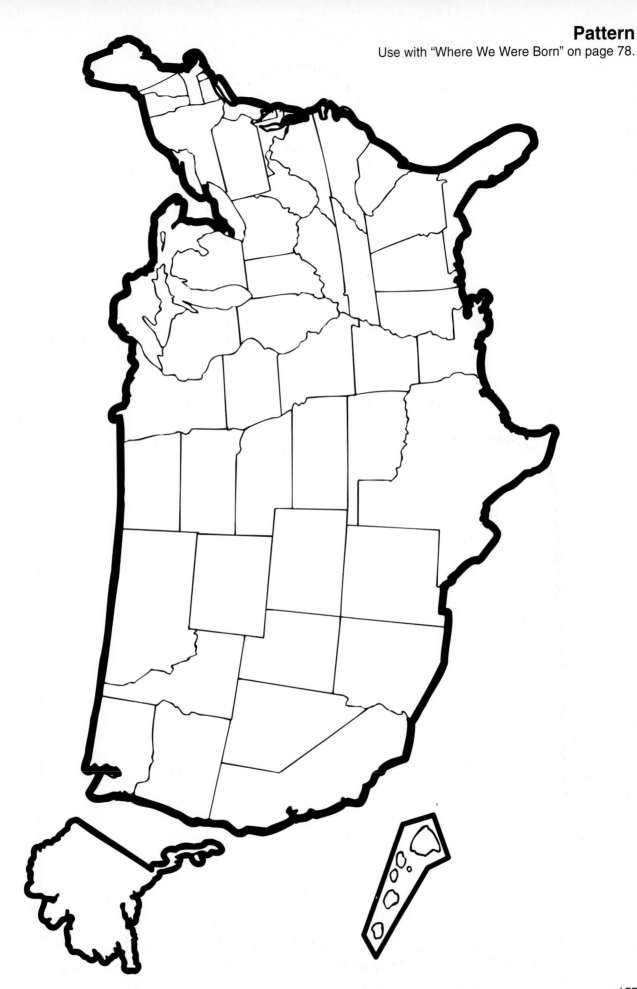

# Patterns
Use with "Don't Monkey Around!" on page 79.

# Index